Arthur Koestler was born in Budapest in 1905 and attended the University of Vienna. He was foreign correspondent for German and British publications and during the Spanish Civil War was captured by the Fascists and condemned to death. Saved by British protests, he came to Britain and has been ever since one of the most interesting and dynamic personalities on the world literary scene. His novel *Darkness at Noon* was translated into thirty-two languages and ranks with Orwell's *Nineteen Eighty-Four* as the most widely read political novel of our time. His other books include *The Thirteenth Tribe, Janus, The Sleepwalkers, The Act of Creation* and *The Ghost in the Machine*—a trilogy on the predicament of man. His latest novel, the first for nineteen years, is *The Call-Girls*.

Arthur Koestler

THE ROOTS OF
COINCIDENCE

with a postscript by Renée Haynes

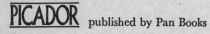 PICADOR published by Pan Books

First published 1972 by Hutchinson & Co Ltd
This Picador edition published 1974 by Pan Books Ltd,
Cavaye Place, London SW10 9PG
5th printing 1979
© Arthur Koestler 1972
ISBN 0 330 24167 2
Printed in Great Britain by
Richard Clay (The Chaucer Press) Ltd, Bungay, Suffolk

To
Rosalind Heywood
Catalyser-in-Chief

"Ladies and gentlemen, I am afraid my subject is rather an exciting one and as I don't like excitement, I shall approach it in a gentle, timid, roundabout way."

Max Beerbohm in a radio broadcast

CONTENTS

I

The ABC of ESP

I

Half of my friends accuse me of an excess of scientific pedantry; the other half of unscientific leanings towards preposterous subjects such as extra-sensory perception (ESP), which they include in the domain of the supernatural. However, it is comforting to know that the same accusations are levelled at an élite of scientists, who make excellent company in the dock.

The accusations are based partly on a legitimate revulsion from superstition and "dabbling with the occult", but mainly on a failure to keep up with recent developments in the exact sciences on the one hand and in parapsychology on the other. Over the last few decades the climate in both camps has significantly changed: parapsychological research has become more rigorous, statistical and computerised, while theoretical physics has become more and more "occult", cheerfully breaking practically every previously sacrosanct "law of nature". Thus to some extent the accusation could even be reversed: parapsychology has laid itself open to the charge of scientific pedantry, quantum physics to the charge of leaning towards such "supernatural" concepts as negative mass and time flowing backwards.

One might call this a negative sort of rapprochement—negative in the sense that the unthinkable phenomena of ESP appear somewhat less preposterous in the light of the unthinkable propositions of physics. I must elaborate a little on these reciprocal developments, starting with the ascent of parapsychology towards scientific respectability.

In 1960 I wrote a series of articles for the London *Observer* on frontiers of research at American universities. Among others, I visited Professor Rhine at Duke University, North Carolina. The passage that follows is the (abbreviated) description of that visit; the reader familiar with developments in ESP research will realise how far things have moved in the ten years that have passed since:

In 1932, Dr. J. B. Rhine, Associate Professor of Psychology, and his wife, Dr. Louisa Rhine, were permitted to establish officially their Parapsychological Laboratory in the Psychology Department headed by Professor William McDougall. It was an event of great symbolic importance: research into the dubious subjects of telepathy and clairvoyance had for the first time been recognised as academically respectable.

Rhine and his collaborators introduced rigorous scientific methods into the investigation of these elusive phenomena. The popular image of the psychic investigator as an uncritical believer and willing prey to fraudulent mediums has become an anachronism. The new school of parapsychology, which Rhine inaugurated, has carried matters to the opposite extreme in its almost fanatical devotion to statistical method, mathematical analysis, mechanised controls. The card-guessing and dice-throwing experiments, repeated over millions of experimental runs with thousands of random experimental subjects—often whole classes of schoolboys who have no idea what the experiment is about; the increasingly elaborate machinery for mechanical card-shuffling, dice-throwing, randomising, recording, and what-have-you, have turned the study of extra-sensory perception into an empirical science as sober, down-to-earth—and all too often as dreary—as training rats to run a maze, or slicing up generations of flatworms. Even the terminology coined by Rhine: ESP, Psi effect, decline effect, reinforcement, BM (blind matching), BT (basic theory), SO (stimulus object), STM (screen touch match), and so forth, is characteristic of the antiseptic atmosphere in modern ESP labs. This New Look in parapsychology is partly a reflection of the prevailing fashion in research in general, but there is also an element in it of bending over backwards to disarm suspicions and to meet the sceptic on his own empirical-statistical ground.

On the whole this sober, functional approach proved effective. Not only several universities, but such conservative bodies as the Royal Society of Medicine, the American Philosophical Association, the Rockefeller, Fulbright and Ciba Foundations, have organised lectures and symposia on parapsychology. The majority of academic psychologists remained hostile, although the giants had always taken telepathy and allied phenomena for granted—from Charcot and Richet through William James to Freud and Jung. Freud thought that telepathy entered into the relations between analyst and patient, and Jung has coined a new name for that old phenomenon: Synchronicity. However, these men belonged to a mellower generation, and formed their conclusions before Rhine put parapsychology "on the map"; among the younger lights, the attitude of H. J. Eysenck is significant. Professor Eysenck occupies the Chair in Psychology at the University of London, and is Director of the Psychological Department at the Maudsley and Bethlem Royal Hospitals. Those acquainted with his work will hardly accuse him of a lack of scepticism or an excess of humility. His summing up of the problem of telepathy commands some interest:

"Unless there is a gigantic conspiracy involving some thirty University departments all over the world, and several hundred highly respected scientists in various fields, many of them originally hostile to the claims of the psychical researchers, the only conclusion the unbiased observer can come to must be that there does exist a small number of people who obtain knowledge existing either in other people's minds, or in the outer world, by means as yet unknown to science. This should not be interpreted as giving any support to such notions as survival after death, philosophical idealism, or anything else. . . ."[1]

In one sense, therefore, it can be said that the Rhines' pioneering work has succeeded. But there is another side to the picture: they are resigned to the periodic storms of defamation that break over their heads every two or three years. The critics fall into two main categories: the first one might call the "insatiable perfectionists" who attack mainly the earlier work on ESP when experimental controls were not as rigorous as they are today; and the *a priorists,* who argue that ESP is a highly improbable hypothesis; that the hypothesis of fraud is easier to fit into the accepted framework of science; and that accordingly, by applying Occam's razor, one must accept the hypothesis of fraud. To this they usually add: "No personal offence meant, we are merely engaged in an exercise in logic." To quote Professor Eysenck again:

"Scientists, especially when they leave the particular field in which they have specialised, are just as ordinary, pig-headed and unreasonable as anybody else, and their unusually high intelligence only makes their prejudices all the more dangerous. . . ."[2]

2

The above was written in 1960. In the decade that has passed since, the situation has changed. Rhine is looked upon as a patriarch; although the "insatiable perfectionists" did succeed in detecting flaws in his early experiments, his integrity is beyond dispute. Instead of "some thirty University departments" at the time when Eysenck wrote, there is now hardly a country in the world which does not have one or several university departments engaged in parapsychological research—with Russia leading the field; and the hypothesis of a "gigantic conspiracy" would have to involve not several hundred but thousands of respectable scientists. In 1967 the New York Academy of Science held a symposium on parapsychology. In 1969 the American Association for the Advancement of Science (the equivalent of the British Association) approved the application of the Parapsychology Association to become an affiliate of that august body. Two previous applications had been rejected; the approval of the third was a sign of the times, and for parapsychology the final seal of respectability.

But the most surprising developments took place in the Soviet Union. One would have thought that parapsychology would be regarded there as a mortal heresy and betrayal of the materialist creed. However, as early as 1916 the great Bechterev, associate of Pavlov, started experiments in ESP; he called it "biological radio", which partly explains how he got away with it. Still, he and his colleagues had to keep pretty quiet about what they were doing. But in the early sixties a sudden change occurred. Leonid Vassiliev, Professor of Physiology at Leningrad University, a student of Bechterev's, published reports of some remarkable experiments in tele-hypnosis. He claimed that hypnotised subjects had been made to awaken from trance by a telepathically transmitted command from a distance; and that hypnotised subjects standing upright were made to fall down by the same means. This was followed by other experiments in telepathic communication between distant towns, such as Moscow and Leningrad, carried out *en masse* with thousands of subjects. The number of scientific publications on parapsychology in Soviet Russia, which in 1958 had amounted to two, had by 1967 increased to thirty-five per year, and in 1969 to seventy; while the number of publications *against* parapsychology in 1958 had been one, and in 1969 four.[3] Since in the USSR all publications are state-controlled, the sudden boom in parapsychology was obviously supported, or inspired, from higher quarters. The motives for it can be guessed from Vassiliev quoting in one of his first publications "an eminent Soviet rocket pioneer" to the effect that "the phenomena of telepathy can no longer be called into question". This conveyed to any Soviet scientist trained to read between the lines that ESP, once its technique has been mastered and made to function reliably, might have important strategic uses as a method of direct communication. This seemingly fantastic idea was confirmed as far back as 1963 by a high official of NASA, the American National Aeronautics and Space Administration:*

A concentrated effort towards a highly interesting problem in modern science—the nature and essence of certain phenomena of electro-magnetic [sic] communication between living organisms—is reportedly being pursued with top priority under the Soviet-manned space programme. Until recently these phenomena have in general been ignored by Western scientists; however, the many hypotheses involved are now receiving attention in world literature.

Specific US experiments in energy transfer phenomena, or the relationship between the physical fields of particles and the non-demonstrable "personal" psi-plasma field [sic], are being carried out or planned under various advanced concepts.

... To Western scientists and engineers the results of valid experimentation in energy transfer could lead to new communications media and advanced emergency techniques, as well as to biocybernetical aids for integrating with a conceptual design of an ultimate operational flight system.

Such a design could result from a present NASA study on data subsystems and certain astronaut self-contained sensor systems.

Dr. Konecci then confirmed that both NASA and the Soviet Academy of Sciences were actively engaged in the study of telepathic phenomena (to which he coyly referred as "energy transfer" or "psycho-physiological information transfer"). He commented:

* Dr. Eugene B. Konecci, Director, Biotechnology and Human Research, Office of Advanced Research and Technology, in the National Aeronautics and Space Administration, speaking at the Fourteenth International Astronautics Federation meeting (Paris, September 26 to October 1).

This vitally important OART [Office of Advanced Research and Technology] study involves the function of the psycho-physiological information acquisition, processing and control systems.[4]

That ESP should be transmitted by electro-magnetic waves is, as we shall see, a most unlikely hypothesis; and what a "personal psi-plasma field" means is anybody's guess. However, there can be little doubt that certain NASA agencies are taking the possibilities of telepathic communication as seriously as their opposite numbers in the Soviet Union. But they are understandably reluctant to talk about it—perhaps for fear of ridicule, perhaps for "security reasons"—and thus the public was rather startled to learn, a few months after the Apollo 14 mission to the moon in February 1971, that astronaut Mitchell had attempted during the flight to establish telepathic contact with four selected subjects on earth. The experiments followed Professor Rhine's classic procedures in card-guessing, and Captain Mitchell then visited Rhine at Duke University to analyse the results. At the time of writing the results have not been published, but Press reports* quoted Captain Mitchell's statement that they were "far exceeding anything expected".

The father of cybernetics, Norbert Wiener, also employed a discreet terminology when he prophesied that the study of telepathy would become an integral part of psychology in the future:

Many other considerations which up to the present have been situated in a somewhat shameful background, such as the study of direct communication at a distance, possibly by some sort of radiative phenomenon, are going to be subjected to a real trend in scientific examination, which will not be corrupted by the unscientific assumption that we are

* e.g., in the *International Herald Tribune*, June 23, 1971.

18

dealing with phenomena with no physical correlates.[5]

Needless to say, a number of scientists maintain a hostile attitude, though they admit being impressed by the evidence. Perhaps the most bellicose among them is Professor Hansel, who recently made a sort of last-ditch stand on the conspiracy of fraud theory.* Another psychologist wrote in the American journal *Science* that "not a thousand experiments with ten million trials and by a hundred separate investigators" could make him accept extra-sensory perception. In a similar vein the Professor of Psychology at McGill University, D. O. Hebb, a leading behaviourist, frankly declared that he rejected the evidence for telepathy, strong though it was, "because the idea does not make sense"—admitting that this rejection was "in the literal sense just prejudice".[6] The mathematician Warren Weaver, one of the founders of modern communication theory, was equally sincere: "I find this [ESP] a subject that is so intellectually uncomfortable as to be almost painful. I end by concluding that I cannot explain away Professor Rhine's evidence, and that I also cannot accept his interpretation."[7]

Yet on the whole the opposition is diminishing, and one can detect a subtle change in these negative utterances from the aggressive and cock-sure to the almost apologetic. At the same time, the number of those who consider ESP—to quote the conservative *New Scientist*—"as a speculative but potentially important area of investigation"[8] is steadily growing and includes an impressive list of Nobel laureates in physics and medicine, professors of philosophy, fellows of the Royal Society and the Soviet Academy of

* C. E. M. Hansel, *ESP: A Scientific Evaluation*, London, 1966. Regarding the "Hansel controversy", see for instance, Professor C. D. Broad's *Lectures on Psychical Research* (Routlege & Kegan Paul, 1962), Appendix to Chapter III; Gertrude Schmeidler, *Extra-Sensory Perception* (Atherton Press, 1969), and Sir Cyril Burt in *Science and ESP*, ed. J. R. Smythies (Routledge & Kegan Paul, 1967).

Science. One can almost foresee the time when ESP will be the fashionable craze in science, and the latest ESP-recording gadgets will replace the rat-conditioning boxes in the laboratories. To return to an earlier metaphor, the dock for the accused might be changing into a bandwagon.

3

And yet in Warren Weaver's words the "almost painful intellectual discomfort" about telepathy and kindred phenomena persists not only in the minds of the sceptical opposition but also of those who were reluctantly brought to recognise the reality of these phenomena—either by the experimental evidence or under the direct impact of some personal experiences, or both. The emphasis is on "reluctantly", and the remarks that follow apply to this category only; the "born believer" does not feel that intellectual discomfort and takes the phenomena for granted, whether they can be rationally explained or not. But for the reluctant converts—to which category I also belong—it is harder. As a friend of mine, a science editor, remarked: "ESP is a pain in the neck. I would be happier without it; but it is there."

I shall try to enumerate briefly some of the irritants which seem to cause, or contribute to, that painful discomfort. First, vaguely remembered tales of fraudulent mediums who disgorge ectoplasmic phantoms made of cheesecloth, and speak in the voices of the departed or convey their messages by automatic writing. However, parapsychology is quite a different matter from spiritualism, and the latter is beyond the scope of this essay. But it is only fair to point out that while many professional mediums were fraudulent, there have been a few cases of "automatic scripts", written by non-professionals of undoubted integrity, which are something of a puzzle and have been the subject of protracted academic controversies.* The most comfortable explanation appears to be that the writers were victims of self-deception, mistaking the productions of their subconscious minds for messages from the beyond.

The whole subject of mediumship was bedevilled by the extreme difficulty of drawing a neat line between deliberate swindle, unconscious self-deception, and sporadic cheating on bad days. However, the controlled laboratory experiments of modern ESP research are designed to exclude deception—conscious or unconscious—as far as humanly possible; and the controls are as rigorous, sometimes even more so, as in any other field of research. But the lore of the past, of funny goings-on in the darkened Victorian parlour, is still a contributory factor to intellectual discomfort. It is aggravated by the fact that "sensitives" are by definition sensitive—more emotional than rational, often unpredictable, sometimes of hysterical disposition.†

* The most celebrated case is perhaps that of Mrs. Winifred Coombe-Tennant, the first woman appointed by the British Government as a delegate to the Assembly of the United Nations, who acted as a medium and produced automatic scripts under the pen name of Mrs. Willett. This was a closely guarded secret, unknown even to her family. Readers interested in this story, with many ramifications involving the former Prime Minister, Lord Balfour, and other eminent personalities, are referred to *The Palm Sunday Case: New Light on an Old Love Story* by the Countess of Balfour (Proceedings, SPR, Vol 52, Part 189, February 1960); *The Sixth Sense* by Rosalind Heywood (London, 1959); and *Swan on a Black Sea* by Geraldine Cummings (London, 1st Edition, 1965, revised Edition 1970).

† Professor Burt, in his 1968 Myers Memorial Lecture,[9] has an illuminating footnote on this:

"A number of investigations have shown that the analytic, intellectual mind of the civilised adult seems peculiarly resistant to all types of paranormal cognition. One of the most recent researches is that of Robert and Henie Brier, who tested several samples of people belonging to a society known as Mensa: here the sole qualification for membership is an IQ within the top two per cent of the popu-

The next factor of discomfort is a rather sad paradox: I have already hinted at it. A century ago, enlightened people were repelled by the occult melodrama of spiritualistic séances; today one is put off by the sterilised atmosphere in the parapsychological laboratory, with its forbidding gadgets, the monotonous series of mechanised card-guessing experiments, and the complex mathematics involved in the evaluation of the results. The statistical methods of modern parapsychology reflect the statistical orientation in the other sciences, but that does not make them more palatable to ordinary mortals.

Nor are the results very convincing, except to the mathematically minded. The first approach to telepathy of Rhine and his school was through card-guessing experiments. They used specially manufactured cards, so-called Zener cards, which had only five markings: circle, square, cross, star, waves. The "sender" or "agent" turned up card after card screened from view, and the "percipient" or "receiver" tried to guess telepathically which of the five cards the agent was looking at. The guesses were recorded, and after a suitable number of tries (which might go on for an hour or two), the results were evaluated. The probability of a correct guess made by pure chance was obviously one in five, i.e. twenty hits in a hundred tries. Now one of the cornerstones of the theory of probability, and of modern physics in general, is the "law of large numbers" which states, in simplified form, that the larger the number of tries the closer the ratio of hits to misses will approach chance expectation—and, con-

lation. In all the tests of ESP their average score was significantly *less* than that expected by chance. Incidentally this type of research emphasises the fact that the absence of successful guesses is not necessarily just a negative result: it is always important to note the occurrence of a disproportionate number not only of 'psi-hits', but also of 'psi-misses'" (R. and H. Brier, "ESP Experiments with High IQ Subjects", ap. J. B. Rhine and R. Brier, *Parapsychology Today*, 1968).

versely, the larger the number of tries, the greater the odds against persistent deviations from that ratio. If significant deviations from chance expectation nevertheless do persist in a series of, say, several thousand tries, then the only reasonable—and scientific—conclusion is that some factor other than chance must be operating to account for the result. And since the experimental set-up excludes any sensory perception of the "target card" by the guessing subject, one must conclude that his persistent high scoring is due to some form of extra-sensory perception. This, from the point of view of scientific methodology, is strictly orthodox, inductive reasoning; and this is what convinced so many sceptics, particularly physicists, that ESP is a hard reality.

The odds against chance, which the experiments by Rhine and his English followers demonstrated, were indeed astronomical—of the order of millions, and even higher.* Thus, according to the rules of the game in the exact sciences, the question "Does ESP exist?" should have been regarded as settled, and the controversy should have shifted to the next problem, "How does it work?"

And yet the malaise persisted. For one thing, guessing card after card a hundred, a thousand times is a very monotonous and boring exercise; even the most enthusiastic experimental subjects showed a marked decline in hits towards the end of each session, and after some weeks or months of intense experimenting most of them lost altogether their special gifts. Incidentally, this "decline effect" (from the beginning to the end of a session) was considered as additional proof that there was some human factor at work influencing the scores, and not just chance.

Nevertheless there was, as already said, something profoundly unsatisfactory in the experimental design to

* Among English experimenters the most impressive results were achieved by the eminent Cambridge psychologist Thouless, and the mathematician Dr. Soal.

all but the mathematically minded. An example will illustrate this. A subject in an ESP test makes a series of a hundred successive guesses at a hundred consecutive cards (which the experimenter turns up one by one in a different room or a different building). Since there are five types of cards, his chance expectation is one correct guess in five or twenty correct guesses in a hundred tries. Assuming he has made twenty-two, instead of twenty correct guesses—nobody will turn a hair. The experiment continues until the subject has made a thousand guesses— and he again does ten per cent better than chance expectation: two hundred and twenty hits instead of two hundred. Here, as the universally accepted probability calculus (based on the so-called binomial formula) shows, the odds against such a result occurring by pure chance are six to one. The subject carries on to five thousand guesses, and continues to score ten per cent over average: eleven hundred hits instead of a thousand. The odds against chance are now two thousand against one. Relentlessly he carries on until he has made ten thousand guesses—and lo, he scored two thousand two hundred instead of two thousand hits. The odds for this being the work of pure chance are now one in two million.

Such is the "law of great numbers". To the mathematician and physicist it is an elementary tool; to the non-mathematician the steep rise of the odds against chance is a paradox and an added source of intellectual discomfort. The nearest one can get to an intuitive grasp of the paradox is by reflecting that if that ten per cent deviation from average, however trivial in itself, keeps stubbornly persisting on and on to a thousand, five thousand, ten thousand tries, then it stands to reason that there must be a reason for it. And that is all that the probability calculus is meant to prove. The first published results by Rhine in 1934 contained the complete record of eighty-five thousand card-calling tries, conducted with a number of selected subjects.* The overall score averaged twenty-eight hits instead of twenty in a hundred guesses. The odds against this are, as already said, astronomical, and this was in fact the first important break-through of ESP into respectability.

And yet there is to the non-mathematician something profoundly disturbing in the idea that an average of twenty-eight correct guesses instead of twenty should have such momentous results, even when very large numbers are involved. The mathematically naive person seems to have a more acute awareness than the specialist of the basic paradox of probability theory, over which philosophers have puzzled ever since Pascal initiated that branch of science (for the purpose of improving the gambling prospects of a philosopher friend, the Chevalier de Méré). The paradox consists, loosely speaking, in the fact that probability theory is able to predict with uncanny precision the overall outcome of processes made up out of a large number of individual happenings, each of which in itself is unpredictable. In other words, we observe a large number of uncertainties producing a certainty, a large number of chance events creating a lawful total outcome.

But, paradoxical or not, it works. In thermodynamics we can predict exactly the temperature of a gas under a given pressure, although the gas molecules, whose speed determines the temperature, all fly about, collide and rebound in their crazy ways like a swarm of gnats on an LSD trip. The archaeologist who determines the age of a fossil by the radio-carbon test relies on the fact that radioactive substances decompose at a rigorously fixed rate (their so-called "half-life"†), although the disintegration

---

* The record included the scores of subjects who had been rejected after a preliminary try because their scores were average or *below*.
† i.e. the time it takes for half of the atoms of a given radio-active substance to decay.

of their individual atoms is spontaneous and unpredictable even in theory. In sub-atomic physics in general, Heisenberg's Uncertainty Principle and the laws of quantum mechanics have replaced causality by probability. In genetics, ever since Abbot Mendel started counting his dwarf peas, the statistical approach reigns supreme. And so it does in the more mundane spheres of the insurance business and gambling casinos. None of them could survive if the laws of chance were not so paradoxically reliable.

A classical example of statistical wizardry concerns the death of soldiers kicked by cavalry horses in the German Army from 1875 to 1894. The total number of deaths in fourteen army corps over these twenty years was 196. A German mathematician undertook to calculate from these data alone the theoretical frequency of zero, one, two or more deaths per army corps per year.* The comparison between theoretical and actual figures reads:

Number of deaths per army corps per year	Actual number of instances	Theoretical number of instances
0	144	139·0
1	91	97·3
2	32	34·1
3	11	8·0
4	2	1·4
5 or more	0	0·2

After Warren Weaver[10]

To make this somewhat involved table clearer: how often in these twenty years would any of the fourteen army corps suffer two çasualties in a single year? The theory says that this should occur 34·1 times. In fact it occurred thirty-two times. All the mathematician had to go on for his calculations was the total number of casualties

* He used the so-called Poisson distribution, derived from the more widely used Gaussian curve.

in $14 \times 20 = 280$ "army corps years". From this single datum he was able to deduce with the aid of Poisson's equation the relative frequency of 0, 1, 2, 3 or 4 casualties suffered by a single army corps in a single year.

Another mystery of the theory of chance is reflected in the following quotation from Warren Weaver:

The circumstances which result in a dog biting a person seriously enough so that the matter gets reported to the health authorities would seem to be complex and unpredictable indeed. In New York City, in the year 1955, there were, on the average, 75·3 reports per day to the Department of Health of bitings of people. In 1956 the corresponding number was 73·6. In 1957 it was 73·2. In 1957 and 1958 the figures were 74·5 and 72·6.[11]

Weaver comments:

One of the most striking and fundamental things about probability theory is that it leads to an understanding [sic] of the otherwise strange fact that events which are individually capricious and unpredictable can, when treated en masse, lead to very stable *average* performances.[12]

But does it really lead to an *understanding*? How do those German Army horses adjust the frequency of their lethal kicks to the requirements of the Poisson equation? How do the dogs in New York know that their daily ration of biting is exhausted? How does the roulette ball know that in the long run zero must come up once in thirty-seven times, if the casino is to be kept going? The soothing explanation that the countless minute influences on horses, dogs or roulette balls must in the long run "cancel out", is in fact begging the question. It cannot answer the hoary paradox resulting from the fact that the outcome of the croupier's throw is not causally related to the outcome of previous throws: that if red came up twenty-eight times in a row (which, I believe, is the longest series ever recorded), the chances of it coming up yet once more are still fifty-fifty.

Probability theory is the offspring of paradox wedded to mathematics. But it works. The whole edifice of modern physics relies on it, the geneticist relies on it, the archaeologist relies on it, business relies on it. And it works, to say it once more, with uncanny accuracy where large numbers of events are considered *en masse*. That precisely is the reason why, when a large series of events persistently deviates from chance expectation, we are driven to the conclusion that some factor other than chance is involved.

We are driven to it, but we are not happy about it. If card-guessing were all there is to parapsychology, it would hardly be worth while to bother about it. At the same time, however, the statistical results obtained in the experiments by Rhine, Soal, Thouless and so on, constitute the strongest evidence to confound the sceptical scientist. One way of convincing a deaf person that a gramophone emits music is to show him the grooves on the record through a magnifying glass.

Another intuitive objection to card-guessing, and statistical experiments in general, could be expressed as follows: "All right, your telepathic subject scores on the average eight hits out of twenty-five guesses, instead of the chance expectation of five hits. This is very impressive, but it still leaves him with seventeen misses out of twenty-five. Assuming that the persistent excess is due to ESP, it must be a very erratic faculty if it just goes on and off—and mostly off."

This is certainly true. One could object that the single

molecules of the vapour in a steam engine, or the particles in an atomic pile, behave just as erratically; only the total outcome is guaranteed, as it were. But the analogy is only partly valid because in ESP experiments not even the total outcome is assured. However promising the subject, however impressive his past scoring record, there is no certainty that at the next experimental session his ESP faculty will work. And this, in fact, is one of the main arguments of the sceptic. One of the fundamental requirements in the exact sciences is that an experiment should be *repeatable* and its outcome *predictable* (within certain statistical limits). But it is in the very nature of parapsychological phenomena that they are *not* repeatable at will, and that they operate unpredictably. This is the issue which has bedevilled the controversy from its very beginnings.

A moment's reflection will show, however, that the sceptic's criticism is unfair. Repeatability and predictability are valid criteria in the physical sciences, but less so on the frontiers of medicine, and even less in those branches of psychology which involve unconscious processes and the autonomic nervous system. Erection of the penis of the human male is, alas, rather unpredictable, and so is the female orgasm. The type of stringent controls applied to ESP experiments, and the presence of sceptical observers, would certainly not facilitate their occurrence. This is not a whimsical analogy, because sex and ESP are both governed by unconscious processes which are not under voluntary control; moreover, attempts to produce them by conscious effort may prove to be self-defeating. For nearly half a century parapsychologists of the statistical school have been hankering after the ideal experiment which would satisfy the strictest criteria of repeatability and predictability. This might turn out to be a will-o'-the-wisp until psychologists discover a technique to induce extra-sensory perceptions at will.

4

A less gruelling approach to parapsychology than card-guessing statistics is indicated by what one might call the "classical" type of experiments carried out in the early days of the British Society for Psychical Research (SPR).

In the 1880's two Liverpool notables, Malcolm Guthrie, a Justice of the Peace and Governor of University College, and James Birchall, a headmaster, carried out a series of 246 experiments in the telepathic transmission of drawings to specially gifted subjects. After publishing their early results in the Proceedings of the Society, they approached Sir Oliver Lodge, one of the outstanding physicists of his time, who was in turn President of the Physical Society, of the British Association, the Radio Society, the Röntgen Society, a Fellow of the Royal Society, and so on. Lodge was persuaded to take charge of the experiments; the following extract from his account may convey something of the atmosphere in which they were carried out:

> If I had merely witnessed facts as a passive spectator I should most certainly not publicly report upon them. So long as one is bound to accept imposed conditions and merely witness what goes on, I have no confidence in my own penetration, and am perfectly sure that a conjuror could impose on me, possibly even to the extent of making me think that he was not imposing on me; but when one has control of the circumstances, can change them at will and arrange one's own experiments, one gradually acquires a belief in the phenomena observed quite comparable to that induced by the repetition of ordinary physical experiments.[13]

The diagram below shows in the top row six drawings, freely improvised by Guthrie and "transmitted" to the percipient "Miss E."; the row below shows her reproductions of them. They are the complete record of a consecutive series of telepathic transmissions during a single experimental session:

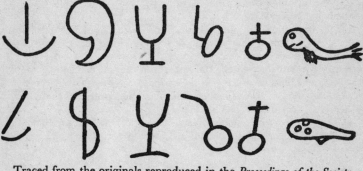

Traced from the originals reproduced in the *Proceedings of the Society for Psychical Research,* Vol. II, 1884 (reduced in scale).

In the same volume of the Proceedings ten more completely successful transmissions of drawings were published. The number of partial successes cannot be expressed in precise figures; by a conservative standard of judging similarities they amount to more than a half out of 246 tries. But in this type of experiment statistics hardly matter. To hit on one card among five possibles is one thing; to reproduce a design out of an infinite number of possible designs is quite another. And Guthrie's experiments were by no means unique; a number of equally impressive results were reported in the early volumes of the *Proceedings of the Society for Psychical Research.*

This may be the place to say a few words about the British Society for Psychical Research. Its character, as well as its academic and social standing, can perhaps be conveyed in the simplest way by the following list of its past presidents, all of whom took an active part in ESP research; they include three Nobel laureates, ten Fellows of the Royal Society, one Prime Minister and a galaxy of professors, mostly physicists and philosophers:

1882–4	Henry Sidgwick, Knightbridge Professor of Moral Philosophy, Cambridge.
1885–7	Balfour Stewart, F.R.S., Professor of Physics, University of Manchester.
1888–92	Henry Sidgwick q.v.
1893	Arthur Earl of Balfour, K.G., O.M. Philosopher. Prime Minister, Foreign Secretary. President of the British Association, etc.
1894–5	William James, Harvard Professor of Psychology and Philosophy.
1896–7	Sir William Crookes, O.M., F.R.S. Discoverer of thallium, inventor of the radiometer, etc.
1900	Frederic W. H. Myers. Classical scholar. Originated concept of subliminal self, coined terms *telepathy, supernormal, veridical.*
1901–3	Sir Oliver Lodge, F.R.S. (see above).
1904	Sir William Barrett, F.R.S., Professor of Physics, Dublin. In 1876 read a paper on telepathy in hypnotised subjects to the anthropological section of the British Association, which refused either to appoint a Committee of Investigation or to publish the paper.
1905	Charles Richet, Professor of Medicine. French physiologist, discovered principle of serum therapy. Nobel Prize (1913) for work on anaphylaxis.
1906–7	Rt. Hon. Gerald Balfour (younger brother of Arthur Balfour q.v.). Fellow of Trinity College, Cambridge. Chief Secretary for Ireland 1895–6. President Board of Trade 1900–5.
1908–9	Mrs. Henry Sidgwick (*née* Eleanor Balfour). First Principal Newnham College, Cambridge 1892–1910.
1910	H. Arthur Smith, M.A., L.L.B. Barrister at law.
1911	Andrew Lang. First Gifford lecturer. Authority on mythology and folklore.
1912	Bishop W. Boyd Carpenter, D.D., K.C.V.O., Bishop of Ripon, Canon of Westminster.
1913	Henri Bergson. Philosopher. Professor at the Sorbonne. Academicien. Nobel Prize 1927.
1914	F. C. S. Schiller. British pragmatist philosopher, Oxford. Professor, University of Los Angeles.
1915–16	Gilbert Murray, LL.D., LITT.D., O.M. Regius Professor of Greek at Oxford.

1917–18   L. P. Jacks, LL.D., D.D. Editor Hibbert Journal. Professor of Philosophy, Manchester College, Oxford.

1919   Lord Rayleigh, O.M., F.R.S. Nobel Prize 1904. Cambridge Professor of Experimental Physics 1879–84. President of the Royal Society. Discovered argon (with Sir William Ramsey).

1920–1   William McDougall, M.SC., M.B., F.R.S. Medical psychologist. Professor of Psychology at Harvard, and later at Duke University, N. Carolina.

1922   T. W. Mitchell, M.D. Editor *British Journal of Medical Psychology*.

1923   Camille Flammarion. French astronomer. Founder and director Juvisy Observatory.

1924–5   J. G. Piddington. Businessman, administrator of the Society's finances.

1926–7   Hans Driesch, Professor of Philosophy, University of Heidelberg. Pioneer of experimental biology.

1928–9   Sir Lawrence Jones Bt., B.A. (Oxon), F.R.S.L.

1930–1   Walter Franklin Prince, PH.D. American lawyer, student of multiple personality.

1932   Mrs. Henry Sidgwick (President of Honour) q.v. jointly with Sir Oliver Lodge q.v.

1933–4   The Hon. Mrs. Alfred Lyttelton (*née* Edith Balfour), D.B.E., G.B.E. Delegate to League of Nations Assembly.

1935–6   C. D. Broad, LITT.D., F.B.A. Knightbridge Professor of Moral Philosophy, University of Cambridge. President Aristotelian Society 1927–8.

1937–8   Lord Rayleigh, F.R.S. Physicist. President of the British Association, son of the third Lord Rayleigh q.v.

1939–41   H. H. Price, F.B.A. Wykeham Professor of Logic at Oxford.*

1942–4   R. H. Thouless, PH.D. Psychologist, University of Cambridge.

1945–6   G. N. M. Tyrrell, B.A. London, Physics and Mathematics. Worked with Marconi on the development of radio.

1947–8   W. H. Salter, LL.B. Classical Scholar.

1949   Gardner Murphy, Professor of Psychology, Harvard.

1950–1   S. G. Soal, M.A., D.SC. Mathematician.

1952   Gilbert Murray, O.M. q.v.

1953–5   F. J. M. Stratton, D.S.O., F.R.S. President Royal Astronomical Association; Professor of Astrophysics, University of Cambridge; Director Solar Physics Observatory, Cambridge.

1956–8   G. W. Lambert, C.B. Assistant Secretary of State, War Office. Originator of the geophysical theory of poltergeists.

1958–60   C. D. Broad q.v.

* Not to be confused with the controversial spiritualist Harry Price.

1960–1   H. H. Price q.v.

1961–3   E. R. Dodds, F.B.A., M.A., D.LITT. Regius Professor of Greek, University of Oxford.

1963–5   D. J. West, M.D., CH.B., D.P.M. Psychiatrist and criminologist.

1965–9   Sir Alister Hardy, F.R.S. Linacre Professor of Zoology, Oxford.

1970   W. A. H. Rushton, F.R.S. Director of Medical Studies, Trinity College, Cambridge. Professor of Visual Physiology, Cambridge University.

1971   C. W. K. Mundle, B.A. (Oxon), M.A. Director, Department of Philosophy, University College of North Wales, Bangor.

If one included the Vice-Presidents and officers of the Society's Council, the list would become even more formidable (e.g. Sir J. J. Thomson, discoverer of the electron). But even in this sketchy form, it ought to be sufficient to demonstrate that ESP research is not a playground for superstitious cranks, and that the idea of a fraudulent conspiracy is absurd.

Among the most successful experimenters of the "pre-statistical" days before the advent of Rhine was Professor Gilbert Murray. For many years he and his circle of distinguished friends played "thought transference" as a kind of parlour game. Murray first reported briefly on these experiments in his Presidential Address to the SPR in 1915, and the last time in his Address of 1952 when he was re-elected as President. Thus the experiments must have continued for at least twenty years. More detailed analyses of them were given by Mrs. A. Verrall (Lecturer in Classics at Newnham College, Cambridge),[14] and by Mrs. Henry Sidgwick in 1924.[15] Throughout the experiments Murray himself acted as percipient, but different members of the group as agents. The opening sentence of Mrs. Sidgwick's report said:

Professor Gilbert Murray's experiments in thought-transference are perhaps the most important ever brought to the notice of the Society. . . . It is surprising,

I think, that they have not attracted more general attention than, so far as I know, they have.

It is indeed. After all, Gilbert Murray was not only the most prominent classical scholar of his time, but a public figure comparable to Bertrand Russell; he drafted the Covenant of the League of Nations, and was showered with honours by learned societies from all over the world. Yet his experiments in telepathy remain practically unknown to this day, and are thus worth a few paragraphs—the more so as they convey a quite different atmosphere from the card-guessing ESP factories. Here are some extracts from his 1952 address:[16]

> Let me say at once that my experiments belong to the pre-statistical stage of psychical research.... Still I do not see how there can have been any significant failure of control.... Fraud, I think, is out of the question; however slippery the behaviour of my subconscious, too many respectable people would have had to be its accomplices.
> ... The method was always the same. I was sent out of the drawing-room either to the dining-room or to the end of the hall, the door or doors, of course, being shut. The others remained in the drawing-room: someone chose a subject which was hastily written down, word for word. Then I was called in and my words written down.

Out of the first five hundred and five experiments, some sixty per cent were considered by the group as evidential, forty per cent as failures. Here are a few examples of "evidential" cases (the protocol indicates first the name of the agent; then the subject which Murray was to guess as it was written down; then Murray's words on being called back to the drawing-room):

COUNTESS OF CARLISLE (agent): "The Crimean soldiers after their return receiving their medals from Queen Victoria at [the] Horse Guards."

PROFESSOR MURRAY: "Is it the King giving V.C.s and things to people? Yes [I] think it's an investiture of some sort."

COUNTESS OF CARLISLE (agent): "Thinking of the *Lusitania*."

PROFESSOR MURRAY: "I have got this violently. I have got an awful impression of naval disaster. I should think it was the torpedoing of the *Lusitania*.

MURRAY'S DAUGHTER, ROSALIND: "I think of dancing with the Head of the Dutch Foreign Office at a *café chantant* at The Hague."

PROFESSOR MURRAY: "A faint impression of your journey abroad. I should say something official; sort of official soirée or dancing or something. Feel as if it was in Holland."

Sometimes the experiments classified as failures are as revealing as the successes:

MARGARET DAVIS (agent): "Medici Chapel and tombs; sudden chill; absolute stillness. Marble figures who seem to have been there all night."

PROFESSOR MURRAY: "I wonder if this is right. I have got a feeling of a scene in my *Nefrekepta*, where the man goes in, passage after passage, to an inner chamber where Nefrekepta is lying dead with the shadows of his wife and child sitting beside him. But I think it's Indian."

Murray comments: "My poem was translated from an Egyptian story; I suppose I felt the subject was not Egyptian."

Earlier in his address he wrote:

Of course, the personal impression of the percipient himself is by no means conclusive evidence, but I do feel there is one almost universal quality in these guesses of mine which does suit telepathy and does not suit any other explanation. They always begin with a vague emotional quality or atmosphere . . . Even in the failures this feeling of atmosphere often gets through. That is, it was not so much an act of cognition, or a piece of information that was transferred to me, but rather a feeling or an emotion; and it is notable that I never had any success in guessing mere cards or numbers, or any subject that was not in some way interesting or amusing.

Let us consider what we mean by telepathy. I believe most of us in this Society are inclined to agree with Bergson that it is probably a common unnoticed phenomenon in ordinary life, especially between intimates. We all know how often two friends get the same thought at the same moment. Tolstoy, the most acute of observers, speaks of "the instinctive feeling with which one human being guesses another's thoughts. . . ."

5

Returning to recent developments in parapsychological research—perhaps the most frequent reports on ESP type phenomena concern telepathic dreams. In the 1960's an enterprising team at the Maimonides Medical Centre in New York (Drs. Stanley Krippner, Montague Ullman and their associates) founded a "dream laboratory" designed to induce telepathic dreams in controlled experiments. The experimental subjects sleep in single rooms at the Centre; before they go to bed they are wired up to a brain-wave recorder (electro-encephalograph, EEG). The agent, in another room, concentrates on some famous picture in front of him, and waits until the EEG record indicates that the sleeping subject has reached the REM ("rapid eye movements") stage, which indicates that he is dreaming; then the agent awakens him and the subject reports his dream—or as much as he can remember of it.

Later on, more elaborate experimental procedures were used: but the paragraph above conveys the gist of them. Unfortunately the similarities between the picture and the reported dream can, once more, only be evaluated by statistical methods; and, however significant the results, they do not carry the same intuitive conviction as, for instance, the Guthrie experiments in which, when the agent drew a cross the subject drew a cross, and when the agent drew a fish the subject drew a fish. But if the picture shows a lake and the subject dreams of a boat or a bath-tub or a fish, the evaluation of "similarity" becomes more complex and less satisfactory, although associative images evoked by telepathy might be considered as remarkable as literal transmissions.

6

The most important source of intellectual discomfort is the argument that ESP cannot exist because it contradicts the laws of physics. If parapsychological phenomena were restricted to telepathy alone, one could probably get around this objection by some sophisticated radiation theory—several of which have actually been proposed by various physicists both in Russia and in the West (see below). But telepathy is not the most puzzling of these phenomena. A number of researchers, starting with Rhine himself, were reluctantly made to realise that some of their star subjects produced results showing more or less the same odds against chance if the target cards to be guessed had *not* been previously seen by the agent. Apparently they did not "read" the agent's thoughts; they seemed to read directly the symbols printed on the cards—including unopened packs fresh from the factory—without the intermediary of another human mind. This phenomenon was labelled "clairvoyance" and defined as "extra-sensory perception of objective events as distinguished from telepathic perception of the mental state of another person". Some form of "mental radio" had always been intuitively acceptable to open-minded persons, trusting that science would sooner or later discover how it worked; the perception-at-a-distance of inanimate objects was much harder to swallow, even with an unprejudiced palate. Gilbert Murray rejected the possibility of clairvoyance; other ESP researchers—for instance Sir Alister Hardy—accepted the evidence for it under protest, as it were. We shall see, however, that other eminent physiologists, such as Sir John Eccles, or psychologists such as Sir Cyril Burt, do not feel the same mental revulsion.

But even worse was to come. In 1934 Dr. Soal, then a lecturer in mathematics at University College, London, read about Rhine's experiments and tried to repeat them. From 1934 to 1939 he experimented with 160 persons who made altogether 128,350 guesses with Zener cards. The result was nil—no significant deviation from chance expectation was found.

"He was about to conclude," Louisa Rhine remarked, "either that the reports from the United States were phoney or else that Englishmen do not have ESP." She went on to suggest that the reason for Soal's failure was lack of emotional involvement on the part of his subjects: 'Soal's subjects came to him mainly in response

39

to advertisements. They were strangers to him, but willing to take the tests that were given in orderly, routine fashion by a careful and earnest experimenter who was doggedly trying to repeat someone else's [i.e. Rhine's] tests. After all, he was not carrying his own torch into the exploration of the unknown. His attempt accordingly was like a car without a sparking plug."[17]

Soal was on the point of giving up in disgust when a fellow researcher, Whately Carington, suggested to him that he check his reports for "displaced" guesses—that is, for hits not on the target card, but on the card which was turned up before it—or *after* it (Carington, who experimented with the telepathic transmission of drawings, thought that he had noticed such displacement effects in some of his subjects). Soal reluctantly undertook the tedious labour of analysing his thousands of columns of experimental protocols, and was both rewarded and disconcerted to find that one of his subjects, Basil Shackleton, had scored consistently on the next card ahead—i.e. precognitively—with results so high that chance had to be ruled out.*

Soal now set out on a new series of experiments with Basil Shackleton, supervised by other experienced researchers from the SPR (so that fraud would have had to involve the collusion of four or more people). The results were statistically so significant that the Professor of Philosophy at Cambridge, C. D. Broad, felt moved to write:

> In my opinion psychical research is highly relevant to philosophy . . . . It will be enough at present to refer to a single instance, viz. Dr. Soal's experiments on card-guessing with Mr. Shackleton as subject, of which I gave a full account in *Philosophy* in 1944. There can

* S. G. Soal and F. Bateman, *Modern Experiments in Telepathy*. Faber & Faber, London, 1954.

be no doubt that the events described happened and were correctly reported; that the odds against chance coincidence piled up to billions to one; and that the nature of the events which involved both telepathy and precognition, conflicts with one or more of the basic limiting principles [of physical science].[18]

One particularly revealing feature transpired during these experiments. The time interval between two guesses which Shackleton found most congenial was 2·6 seconds. At this rate he consistently guessed at the next card to be turned up. If, however, the rate of turning up cards was speeded up to about half that time (an average of 1·4 seconds between guesses), then he guessed just as consistently the card which would turn up *two* ahead. In other words, he was somehow fixated on the event which would occur about two and a half seconds in the future. It should be added that the experiment was so designed that the agent who turned up the cards (in a different room from Shackleton's) could himself not know what the next card or the one after would be; if the agent wished to cheat, he would have to do precognitive cheating. Nor did the order of the cards depend on shuffling the pack. The order was determined by so-called "random number tables"—tables with columns of numbers arranged in a deliberately haphazard order or, rather, lack of order which are prepared by mathematicians for special purposes.

7

But still worse was to come. From the early days at Duke University, in the 1930's, Rhine and his collaborators had experimented with throwing dice and "willing" a certain face to come uppermost. As Louisa Rhine relates, by 1934, after four years of successful experiments with card-guessing, "J. B. Rhine was asking himself, If the mind can know without ordinary means of knowing, can it perhaps also move objects without the ordinary means of moving? In other words, can mind move matter directly[19] [i.e. without apparent transfer of energy]? Certain experiences people occasionally reported suggested that such an effect had occurred. Although such experiences are deeply tinged with the aura of superstition—even more in fact than those that seem to involve ESP—they are occasionally reported in circumstances that raise the question, Could an unknown force have been involved here?"[19a]

She was referring of course to the folklore concerning *Poltergeists*, pictures that fall off the wall, watches that stop at the time of a relative's death, and so on. But the decision to embark on serious research in a territory where angels fear to tread was triggered off by a chance remark one day by a young gambler, "who said that upon occasion when he was properly keyed up, he could make dice fall as he willed".[20]

The dice used in the Duke experiments were either thrown singly or in lots of six; at first by hand from containers, later by electrically-driven rotating cages. The effects of possibly faulty dice were eliminated by concentrating in successive runs of twenty-four throws on each face in turn, so that the effects of bias would cancel out: if a die had a tendency to come to a halt with six uppermost, this had a positive effect when six was the willed target, and an equal negative effect on other runs.

Once more the results seemed to indicate that the dice were influenced by some factor besides chance; but Rhine wisely did not publish them until ten years later, in 1943–4: "it had seemed best to wait a while before throwing a second bombshell".[21] In more than half a million throws the "willed" face came up significantly more often than chance expectation; but there is no point in going into the statistics, which can be found in the original publications.[22] Rhine's experiments were repeated by Haakon Forwald at Duke University, Dr. R. A. McConnell at Pittsburgh University, Dr. R. H. Thouless at Cambridge and G. W. Fisk, a member of the SPR Council, and they all gave positive results (Fisk's subject, in protracted experiments over a period of six years, scored anti-chance odds of fifty thousand to one). This type of effect was labelled PK (psychokinesis) as distinct from ESP (extra-sensory perception); both together are referred to by the blanket name psi: a nice neutral word, signifying the twenty-third letter in the Greek alphabet. To paraphrase Goethe:

> When the mind is at sea
> A new word provides a raft.*

8

Dice-throwing, even by machines, was a primitive procedure which has been replaced by electronic equipment of incomparably greater sophistication. The pioneer of this type of ultra-modern research is Helmut Schmidt,† a brilliant physicist formerly working for the Boeing Scientific Research Laboratories, who became director of the Institute for Parapsychology at Duke University, in succession to Rhine. His original idea was to let subjects predict events on the elementary quantum level initiated by radioactive decay—events which,

---

* *Denn da wo die Begriffe fehlen*
  Stellt ein Wort zur rechten Zeit sich ein.
† His precursors in this field were Beloff and Evans (*JSPR* 1961, 41, and Chauvin and Genthon, *Zeitschrift für Parapsychologie und Grenzgebiete der Psychologie*, 1965, 8).

according to modern physics, are theoretically un-predictable. Since an understanding of the apparatus and procedure requires familiarity with quantum theory, I must confine myself to quoting the Abstract of his first paper,[23] which attracted considerable attention among physicists not otherwise interested in parapsychology.

PRECOGNITION OF A QUANTUM PROCESS

Abstract: In two precognition experiments, the subjects were faced with four coloured lamps which were lit in random sequence. Their objective was to guess which of the four lamps would light up next and to press the corresponding button. In the first experiment, there were three subjects, who carried out a total of 63,066 trials. Their combined results were highly significant ($p < 2 \times 10^{-9}$) [odds against chance two thousand million to one].

In the second experiment, two of the same subjects plus a third had their choice of trying to predict, as before, which lamp would light next (to try for high score) or to choose one which would not light next (low score). In a total of 20,000 trials, the subjects were again successful in achieving their aim to a highly significant extent ($p < 10^{-10}$).

For providing the random target sequence, use was made of single quantum processes which may represent nature's most elementary source of random-ness [the arrival and registration of an electron from a radioactive strontium 90 source]. A practical advan-tage of the device is that it works fast and that the randomness can be easily computer-tested.

The result can be summarised by saying that the subjects made correct predictive guesses at the outcome of theoretically unpredictable sub-atomic processes with a probability against chance of ten thousand million against one.

The next experiment was intended to test whether the subjects could influence random events on the sub-atomic level by a voluntary effort—i.e. by psychokinesis. Again, I must confine myself to Schmidt's summary:

A PK TEST WITH ELECTRONIC EQUIPMENT

Abstract: The subjects in this research were tested for their psychokinetic ability by means of an electronic apparatus made up of a random number generator (RNG) connected with a display panel. The RNG produced random sequences of two numbers which were determined by a simple quantum process (the decay of radioactive strontium-90 nuclei). The essential aspect of the display panel was a circle of nine lamps which lighted one at a time in the clock-wise $(+1)$ direction or the counterclockwise (-1) direction depending on which of the two numbers the RNG produced. The subject's task was to choose either the clockwise or counterclockwise motion and try by PK to make the light proceed in that direction.

One run was made up of 128 "jumps" of the light, and there were four runs per session. In a preliminary series of 216 runs, the 18 subjects had a negative deviation of 129 hits. Accordingly, the main series was expected to give negative scores, and a negative attitude was encouraged among the subjects. Fifteen subjects carried out 256 runs, with a significant negative deviation of 302 hits $(P = \cdot 001)$ [odds against chance 1 in 1,000]. . .[24]

The result of the experiment shows that the binary random number generator had no bias for generation of $+1$'s or -1's as long as it was left unattended (in the randomness tests) but that it displayed a significant bias when the test subjects concentrated on the display panel, wishing for an increased generation rate of one number.

The experiment had been discussed in terms of PK, but in principle the result could certainly also be ascribed to precognition on the part of the experimenter or the subject. Since the sequence of generated numbers depended critically on the time when the test run began, and since the experimenter, in consensus with the subject, decided when to flip the start switch, precognition might have prompted experimenter and subject to start the run at a time which favoured scoring in a certain direction.[25]

The same ambiguity—precognition or psychokinesis—is also present in the first experiment. These phenomena may involve levels where the two become indistinguishable. Our understanding of them is still in the pre-Copernican stage.

In spite of this, the experiments of the new Director of the Duke University Institute seem to have made an even stronger impression on the scientific community than the pioneer work of his predecessor, Professor Rhine—although psychokinesis and precognition are harder to swallow than card-guessing by common or garden telepathy. The impact of Schmidt's work may partly be due to the electronic apparatus he uses, and its completely automated recording devices, which exclude the possibility of human error; but also perhaps to the fact that the experiments operated on the subatomic level, where events are unpredictable in the physicist's own terms, where causal determinism breaks down and 'God plays dice with the universe'. However that may be, Schmidt's experimental reports were published in the most conservative scientific journals, and led to protracted theoretical controversies which are still being pursued as these lines go to the printers.* There has been scepticism, as would be expected, but no open or veiled hints at cheating or 'recording errors'. These have vanished from the controversy—as if an ugly fog had lifted from the landscape.

9

Research in 'classical' telepathy too has at long last moved beyond the card-guessing stage. The most recent experiments, at the time of writing, were undertaken by a group of scientists led by Professor William MacBain at the University of Hawaii. Once more, the London *New Scientist,* though generally opposed to ESP, reported the results in a prominent feature. The following is an extract from its report, dated 20.VIII.1970.

To make a fresh start (and perhaps to confuse the opposition) they [MacBain and his group] have abandoned the term ESP, with its rather negative connotations, and coined the new term quasi-sensory communication, or QSC for short. They also formulated a simple basic hypothesis: "If one individual has access to information not available to another, then under certain circumstances and with known sensory channels rigidly controlled, the second individual can demonstrate knowledge of this information at a higher level than that compatible with the alternative explanation of chance guessing." And then they set out to test it—with most intriguing results.

For their subjects they used 22 volunteer psychology

* Cf., e.g., *New Scientist and Science Journal,* London, June 24, 1971 (article by H. Schmidt on "Mental Influence on Random Events") and subsequent letters in the correspondence columns on July 15, July 29, and August 5, 1971.

students, who operated in pairs . . . The information to be communicated consisted of a set of 23 concepts which seemed likely to evoke a wide range of emotional reactions, and which could be symbolised by simple line drawings (including, for example, home, sleep, sorrow, sunshine, and the Pill). Each pair of students used just five of these concepts. The sender in each pair sat at a row of five display panels, one of which was illuminated for 25 seconds. The receiver faced a similar row of the five symbols, all illuminated, with a button below each. He used the appropriate button to signal the concept he thought had been "transmitted" by the sender. The sender had to concentrate on the illuminated symbol for 25 seconds, and then relax for 5 seconds while the receiver made a choice. Receiver and sender were in separate rooms over 30 feet apart . . .

The actual results . . . were significantly different from . . . random distribution . . . This means that chance guessing alone is not enough to explain the results—a conclusion which receives further support from the finding that certain psychological features of the students correlated with their degree of success as senders or receivers.[26]

10

To conclude this embarrassingly sketchy survey of contemporary parapsychology, it should be pointed out that the quasi-artificial phenomena induced in the laboratory are not necessarily typical of spontaneous ESP experiences encountered in everyday life. Although these do not qualify as scientific evidence—except in well-authenticated cases which are rare—the sheer weight of the material cannot fail to impress. One can classify this so-called "anecdotal material" into several categories, such as: first-hand experiences which, evidence or no evidence, carry the strongest conviction; next, experiences told by other people whose sincerity and critical faculties one trusts, but for which there is no hard proof; third, autobiographical reports which are open to the same objection; and lastly, the hard core of solidly documented cases, investigated by competent researchers.

An early classic example of such a collection is *Phantasms of the Living,* published in 1886, edited by Myers, Guerney and Podmore; among contemporary compilations the most impressive are those of Professor Rhine's wife, Dr. Louisa Rhine, *Hidden Channels of the Mind* (1961) and *ESP in Life and Lab* (1957).

2
*The Perversity of Physics**

I

If the facts reported in the previous section arouse incredulity and a certain intellectual revulsion it is because they seem to contradict what most people believe to be the immutable laws of physics. The main comfort comes from modern physics itself. This is not a paradox, but a consequence of the profound transformation of the physicist's world view, which began in the late nineteenth century and shattered his fundamental concepts of the nature of reality, the meaning of natural law, and the validity of our ideas about space, time, matter and causality. Einstein's writing a preface to Upton Sinclair's *Mental Radio* was a symbolic act; and it is not by chance that so many leading physicists appear among the Presidents and Council members of the Society for Psychical Research. For the deeper the physicist intruded into the realms of the sub-atomic and super-galactic dimensions, the more intensely he was made aware of their paradoxical and commonsense-defying structure, and the more open-minded he became towards the possibility of the seemingly impossible. His own world, based on relativity and quantum theory, is in fact a world of impossibles. Its strange and tantalising flavour is reflected in a remark by J. R. Oppenheimer, Chairman of the Los Alamos project:

* This chapter is rather tough going. Should the stranger to modern physics be baffled by some passages, I hope he will at least gain a general impression of that weird Wonderland.

If we ask . . . whether the position of the electron remains the same, we must say "No"; if we ask whether the electron's position changes with time, we must say "No"; if we ask whether the electron is at rest, we must say "No", if we ask whether it is in motion, we must say "No".[1]

In a similar way Werner Heisenberg, one of the giants of quantum physics, emphasises in his autobiography again and again that "atoms are not *things*. The electrons which form an atom's shells are no longer things in the sense of classical physics, things which could be unambiguously described by concepts like location, velocity, energy, size. When we get down to the atomic level, the objective world in space and time no longer exists, and the mathematical symbols of theoretical physics refer merely to possibilities, not to facts."[2]

Heisenberg will probably go down in history as the man who put an end to causal determinism in physics—and thereby in philosophy—with his celebrated Principle of Indeterminacy (alternatively referred to as the Principle of Uncertainty) for which he got the Nobel Prize in 1931.* The best one can do to convey its meaning to the general reader is by a coarse analogy. A certain static quality of much Renaissance painting is due to the fact that the human figures and their distant background are both in sharp focus—which is optically impossible: when we focus on a close object the background gets blurred, and vice versa. Heisenberg's principle means that in studying the elementary constituents of matter the physicist finds himself in a similar predicament (though of course for different reasons). In classical physics a particle must at

* The reader may find the frequent mention of Nobel awards tiresome. It is intended as a reassurance that some of the strange theories in contemporary physics and psychology discussed in this section were propounded not by cranks but by scientists eminent in their fields.

any time have a definable location and velocity; on the sub-atomic level, however, the situation turns out to be radically different. The more accurately the physicist is able to determine the location of an electron, for instance, the more uncertain its velocity becomes; and vice versa, if he knows its velocity, the location of the electron becomes a blur. This inherent indeterminacy of sub-atomic events is due to the ambiguous and elusive nature of these smallest particles of matter, which in fact are not particles or "things" at all. They are Janus-faced entities which behave under certain circumstances like hard little pellets, under different circumstances, however, like waves or vibrations propagated in a medium devoid of any physical attributes. As Sir William Bragg put it, they seem to be waves on Mondays, Wednesdays and Fridays, and particles on Tuesdays, Thursdays and Saturdays.

At the beginning of this century Lord Rutherford and the great Danish physicist Niels Bohr designed a beguilingly simple model of the atom as a miniature solar system, in which negatively charged electrons circle like planets round a positively charged nucleus. But the model ran into one paradox after another: the electrons behaved quite unlike planets: they kept jumping from one orbit into a different orbit without passing through intervening space—as if the earth were suddenly transferred into the orbit of Mars without having to travel. The orbits themselves were not linear trajectories but wide, blurred tracks, and it was meaningless to ask for instance at what point of its orbit the electron of the hydrogen atom was at any given moment of time; it was equally everywhere. As Bertrand Russell wrote in 1927:

For aught we know an atom may consist entirely of the radiations which come out of it. It is useless to argue that radiations cannot come out of nothing . . . The idea that there is a hard little lump there, which is the electron or proton, is an illegitimate intrusion of commonsense notions derived from touch . . . Matter is a convenient formula for describing what happens where it isn't.[3]

But worse was to come . . . The beautifully simple Rutherford–Bohr model had to be abandoned in favour of a mathematical theory which got rid of the worst paradoxes—but at the price of renouncing any claim of intelligibility or representability in terms of three-dimensional space, time, matter or causation. "The very attempt", Heisenberg wrote, "to conjure up a picture [of elementary particles] and think of them in visual terms is wholly to misinterpret them."[4] Modern physics seems to obey the Second Commandment: "Thou shalt not make unto thee any graven image"—either of gods or of protons.

In his *The Nature of the Physical World* (1928) Sir Arthur Eddington introduced his famous "parable of the two writing desks". One is the antique piece of furniture on which his elbows solidly rest while writing; the other is the desk as the physicist conceives it, consisting almost entirely of empty space, sheer nothingness, sprinkled with unimaginably tiny specks, the electrons whirling round their nuclei, but separated from them by distances a hundred thousand times their own size. And in between—nothing: apart from those few forlorn specks, the interior of the atom is empty. Eddington concluded:

In the world of physics we watch a shadowgraph performance of familiar life. The shadow of my elbow rests on the shadow-table as the shadow-ink flows over the shadow-paper . . . The frank realisation that physical science is concerned with a world of shadows is one of the most significant of recent advances.[5]

2

But even while these lines were written, the shadow-desk underwent another ghostly transformation. The tiny specks which were supposed to be its ultimate constituents turned out to be not "things" but processes—rather analogous to the vibrations of wind instruments. These "matter-waves" were first postulated by the Prince de Broglie—a lover of chamber music—to get over the difficulties into which the Bohr model of the atom had run; the mathematical theory of "wave mechanics" was shortly afterwards formulated by the Austrian Erwin Schrödinger,* and given its final form by the Englishman Paul Dirac.

But, as already said, if the constituents of matter behaved as unsubstantial waves, they also behaved in other circumstances as massive particles. "The electron", de Broglie proclaimed, "is at once a corpuscle and a wave."[6] This dualism, which is fundamental to modern physics, Bohr called the "Principle of Complementarity". "Complementarity" became a kind of credo with the so-called "Copenhagen School"—the dominant school in theoretical physics founded by Bohr. Heisenberg, one of the pillars of that school, commented: "The concept of complementarity is meant to describe a situation in which we can look at

* De Broglie got his Nobel Prize in 1929, Schrödinger in 1931. Both played a part in my life. As a foreign correspondent in Paris I had the privilege of obtaining the first interview with de Broglie a few hours after he got the prize. As a result of that interview, I was appointed Science Editor of the Ullstein chain of Continental newspapers, for whom I worked at the time. Schrödinger I knew first in Berlin before the war; then in 1957 we met again and became close friends; until his death in 1961 we both spent the summer months in the Tyrolean mountain village of Alpbach. Owing to Schrödinger's presence, Alpbach became a place of pilgrimage for theoretical physicists.

one and the same event through two different frames of reference. These two frames mutually exclude each other, but they also complement each other, and only the juxtaposition of these contradictory frames provides an exhaustive view of the appearances of the phenomena."[7] In another place he made a remark which illuminates one of the reasons for our present excursion into nuclear physics: "What the Copenhagen School calls complementarity accords very neatly with the Cartesian dualism of matter and mind."[8]

The same idea was expressed earlier on by Wolfgang Pauli, another giant of the quantum theory, about whom we shall hear more later:

> The general problem of the relationship between mind and body, between the inward and the outward, cannot be said to have been solved by the concept of psycho-physical parallelism postulated in the last century. Modern science has perhaps brought us nearer to a more satisfactory understanding of this relationship, by introducing the concept of complementarity into physics itself. It would be the more satisfactory solution if mind and body could be interpreted as complementary aspects of the same reality.[9]

This, together with the constant emphasis on the theme "atoms are not things"; "on the atomic level the objective world ceases to exist", is suggestive of that post-materialistic trend in modern physics which enticed many physicists into a flirtation with parapsychology—or at least into a tolerant attitude towards it. The connection will become clearer after a few more glimpses at the Wonderland of elementary particles.

3

The field equations of the electron, which treated the constituents of the material world as wave-functions, were beautifully confirmed by experiment. The theory worked. But it worked at the price of accepting its inherent contradictions. The new term "complementarity" became another verbal raft for the mind at sea. When an electron collided with another particle, it behaved more or less like a tiny cannon ball. But when an electron was fired at a screen with two holes in it, it produced the characteristic interference patterns which result when two wave-fronts meet (e.g. after dropping two stones into a pond). Are we to conclude that the single electron passed through *both* holes at the same time? Sir George Thomson, one of those who performed this now classic experiment, commented in his 1960 Presidential Address to the British Association: "[Commonsense would make one expect that] if a particle crosses a flat screen with two holes in it, it must have gone through one to the exclusion of the other. This is not true of an electron."[10]* Sir Cyril Burt wrote about this fundamental paradox in more caustic terms: "If we attempt to describe the apparent behaviour of a single electron when fired at a thin screen of metal containing two minute holes, we should be constrained to infer that the particle passed through the screen in two places at once—a feat which has never yet (as far as I am aware) been performed by the ghosts of either folklore or psychical research."[11]

The alternative explanation was that the electron, while passing through the two holes, transformed itself from a corpuscle into a wave; while in other situations it sort of "condensed" from a wave into a corpuscle. But that of

* One may add for the sake of piquancy that it was Sir George Thomson's father—Sir Joseph J. Thomson—who in the late 1890's discovered the electron; and that he was one of the earliest members of the Society for Psychical Research.

course is just playing with words. The only certainty gained was that the elementary constituents of matter—electrons, protons, even whole atoms—could behave like waves when they did not happen to behave like particles.

Though the constituents of matter could be described with great mathematical accuracy as patterns of vibrations, the question remained—what was it that vibrated? On the one hand, these matter-waves produced physically real phenomena, such as interference patterns on a screen, or the currents in a transistor radio. On the other hand, the whole conception of matter-waves excludes by definition any medium with physical attributes as a carrier of the waves. A wave is movement; but what is that something that moves, producing the shadows on Eddington's shadow-desk? Short of calling it the grin of the Cheshire Cat, it was named the "psi field" or "psi function". Henry Margenau, Professor of Physics at Yale University, recently commented:

> Towards the end of the last century the view arose that all interactions involved material objects. This is no longer held to be true. We now know that there are fields which are wholly non-material. The quantum mechanical interactions of physical psi fields— interestingly and perhaps amusingly the physicist's psi has a certain abstractness and vagueness of interpretation in common with the parapsychologist's psi— these interactions are wholly non-material, yet they are described by the most important and the most basic equations of present-day quantum mechanics. These equations say nothing about masses moving; they regulate the behaviour of very abstract fields, certainly in many cases non-material fields, often as tenuous as the square root of a probability.[12]

Yet the paradox of the physicist's psi field as an immaterial substratum of matter is merely a more esoteric repetition of the earlier paradoxes of the electro-magnetic and gravitational fields. Light, and all other electro-magnetic radiations, including the domesticated radio waves of the mass media, display the same dual character of little pellets of concentrated energy—photons—and of waves in a non-medium devoid of any physical properties. It was once called the ether, but the term was dropped as meaningless, since a medium devoid of physical properties is not a medium. The term "field" was then introduced as another verbal raft, to refer to the de-materialised ether. Mass had already been shown to be the equivalent of concentrated packages of energy, according to Einstein's formula $E = mc^2$ (which yielded the atom bomb as a side-product); and in the general theory of relativity, mass, inertia and gravity had all been reduced to stresses, warps or kinks in empty, multi-dimensional space. The non-things of quantum theory and wave mechanics are thus not isolated curiosities in modern physics, but the culmination of a development which started towards the end of the last century. Sir James Jeans summed it up in a memorable passage in his Rede Lectures:

> Today there is a wide measure of agreement, which on the physical side of science approaches almost to unanimity, that the stream of knowledge is heading towards a non-mechanical reality; the universe begins to look more like a great thought than like a great machine.[13]

The second half of this sentence, after the semi-colon, might strike one as a *non sequitur* or just a poetic metaphor. But the idea goes deeper. The contents of conscious experience have no spatio-temporal dimensions; in this respect they resemble the non-things of quantum physics which also defy definition in terms of space, time and substance—or, to quote Jeans again, can only be described "by going outside space and time". But the unsubstantial contents of consciousness are somehow linked with the substantial brain; and the physicist's unsubstantial psi fields are somehow linked with the substantial aspects of material particles. This is the parallel implied in Heisenberg's remark that the Copenhagen complementarity of corpuscle and wave, and the Cartesian dualism of matter and mind, agree with each other "very neatly"; and in Jeans' remark that the universe looks more like a thought than a machine. "More" and not "equally"—because both in Einstein's cosmos and the sub-atomic micro-cosmos, the non-substantial aspects dominate; in both, matter dissolves into energy, energy into shifting configurations of something unknown. Eddington summed it up in his epigram: "The stuff of the world is mind-stuff." The hard, tangible appearance of things exists only in our medium-sized world measured in pounds and yards, to which our senses are attuned. On both the cosmic and the sub-atomic scale this intimate, tangible relationship turns out to be an illusion.*

* I cannot resist quoting another illuminating footnote from Sir Cyril Burt's essay on "Psychology and Parapsychology":[14]

"How remote the basic constructs of modern physics are from the observable contents of sensory experience is shown by the history of 'energy' and Einstein's unexpected identification of it with 'matter' or 'mass'. . . . A psychologist may be permitted to suggest that the old distinction between matter and energy resulted from the way biological needs determined the evolution of our senses. Our tactile perception of the gravitational effects of mass (e.g. a grain of sand falling on the skin) requires a stimulus of at least $0 \cdot 1$ gram, say about 10^{20} ergs; the kinaesthetic sense (e.g. lifting a weight) is coarser still. On the other hand, the eye in rod-vision is sensitive to less than 5 quanta of radiant energy, about 10^{-10} ergs or rather less. In detecting energy therefore man's perceptual apparatus is 10^{30} times more sensitive than it is in detecting mass. Had the perception of mass been as delicate as the perception of energy, the identity of the two would have seemed self-evident instead of paradoxical. When seeing light we should at the same time have *felt* the pressure or impact of the photons; and mass and energy would from the outset have been regarded as merely two different ways of perceiving the same thing. . . ."

One may add that if our sense of touch were as delicate as our vision, Eddington's solid desk would be nearly (though not quite) transformed into the shadow-desk.

4

In the early 1930's the number of known "elementary particles", which were supposedly the ultimate constituents of matter, was three: the negatively charged electron, the positively charged proton and the chargeless neutron. Protons and neutrons constituted the atomic nucleus, in which practically all the mass of the atom was concentrated; the revolving electrons—or electron-waves—constituted its outer shells. By today we know about a hundred elementary particles, either originating in cosmic radiation or produced in the laboratory. Some of them are extremely short-lived—lasting no longer than an infinitesimal fraction of a second; others, like the photon, have a virtually unlimited life-span. Some of these particles are very odd indeed—one of their quantitative attributes is actually referred to by the technical term "strangeness". Other terms in the vocabulary of modern physics are even odder. M. Gell-Mann has proposed a theory of elementary particles which, with acknowledgements to the Buddha, he called "the eightfold way"; and which enabled him to predict the discovery of yet another previously unknown particle called the omega minus—for which he got the Nobel Prize in 1969. Gell-Mann and his co-workers have even suggested that the "elementary particles" may in fact not be elementary at all, but may consist of even more elementary entities which they decided to call "quarks" —with acknowledgements to James Joyce in *Finnegan's Wake*.* At the time of writing, these hypothetical entities have not, or not yet, been discovered; but "hunting the quark" has become accepted slang in physics laboratories. All of which goes to indicate that theoretical physicists

Quark in German means curds or soft cheese, mostly of an evil-smelling sort.

are well aware of the surrealistic nature of the world they have created.

But it is also a world of great mystery and beauty, reflected in those fantastic photographs of events in the bubble-chamber, which show the trajectories of unimaginably small particles, moving at unimaginable speeds in curves and spirals, colliding, recoiling or exploding and giving birth to other particles or wavicles. The actors in this pageant are invisible, but they leave trails, rows of tiny bubbles in a liquid, loosely comparable to the condensation trails of high-flying jet planes—except that these tracks are sharp, thin lines whose length, angles and curvatures can be measured with sufficient exactitude to determine a particle's energy, speed, electric charge, and so on. This technique enables the physicist to observe the unthinkable—the transformation of mass into energy and of energy into mass. When a photon, a concentrated "package of light", without rest-mass, flies past an atomic nucleus, the photon is converted into an electron and a positron,* both of which have mass, or even into two pairs of them. Vice versa, when an electron and a positron meet they destroy each other, converting their joint masses into high-energy gamma rays. To have penetrated to this depth below the world of appearances is one of the greatest triumphs of human ingenuity. Though the physicists themselves keep warning us that the ghosts we find down there elude the grasp of our understanding, at least we can measure their footprints in the bubble-chamber.

5

Of all the bewildering elementary particles in the physicist's inventory, the most ghost-like is the so-called neutrino. Its existence was predicted in 1930 by Wolfgang

* An electron with a positive charge or anti-electron—see below.

Pauli on purely theoretical grounds, but it was not until 1956, more than twenty-five years later, that actual neutrinos, emanating from the Atomic Energy Commission's huge nuclear piles on the Savannah River, were trapped in the laboratory by F. Reines and C. Cowan. The reason why it took so long to detect them is that the neutrino has virtually no physical properties: no mass, no electric charge, no magnetic field. It is not attracted by gravity, nor captured or repelled by the electric and magnetic fields of other particles while flying past them. Accordingly, a neutrino originating in the Milky Way, or even in some other galaxy, and travelling with the speed of light, can go clean through the solid body of the earth as if it were so much empty space—Eddington's desk, in fact. A neutrino can be stopped only by a direct, head-on collision with another elementary particle, and the chances of such a direct collision, while passing through the whole earth, are estimated at about one in ten thousand million.* "Fortunately", as the science writer Martin Gardner remarks, "there are enough neutrinos around so that collisions *do* occur, otherwise the neutrino would never have been detected. As you read this sentence, billions of neutrinos, coming from the sun and other stars, perhaps even from other galaxies, are streaming through your skull and brain."[15] Not only physicists were excited by the discovery of the neutrino. John Updike, the novelist, wrote a poem to celebrate it, called 'Cosmic Gall':[16]

> Neutrinos, they are very small.
>> They have no charge and have no mass
> And do not interact at all.
> The earth is just a silly ball
>> To them, through which they simply pass,

* Reines and Cowan, the discoverers of the neutrino, have in recent years established laboratories in the depths of salt-mines and gold-mines to trap pure neutrino showers, uncontaminated by other particles from space which cannot penetrate to those depths.

Like dustmaids down a drafty hall
    Or photons through a sheet of glass.
They snub the most exquisite gas,
Ignore the most substantial wall,
    Cold-shoulder steel and sounding brass,
Insult the stallion in his stall,
    And, scorning barriers of class,
Infiltrate you and me! Like tall
And painless guillotines, they fall
    Down through our heads into the grass. . . .

To the unprejudiced mind, neutrinos have indeed a certain affinity with ghosts—which does not prevent them from existing. This is not just a whimsical metaphor. The absence of "gross" physical properties in the neutrino, and its quasi-ethereal character, encouraged speculations about the possible existence of other particles which would provide the missing link between matter and mind. Thus the eminent astronomer V. A. Firsoff suggested that "mind was a universal entity or interaction of the same order as electricity or gravitation, and that there must exist a *modulus of transformation*, analogous to Einstein's famous equality $E = mc^2$, whereby 'mind stuff' could be equated with other entities of the physical world".[17] He further suggested that there may exist elementary particles of the mind-stuff, which he proposed to call "mindons", with properties somewhat similar to the neutrino's:

The universe as seen by a neutrino eye would wear a very unfamiliar look. Our earth and other planets simply would not be there, or might at best appear as thin patches of mist. The sun and other stars may be dimly visible, in as much as they emit some neutrinos . . . A neutrino brain might suspect our existence from certain secondary effects, but would find it very difficult to prove, as we would elude the neutrino instruments at his disposal.

63

Our universe is no truer than that of the neutrinos —they exist, but they exist in a different kind of space, governed by different laws. . . . In our space no material body can exceed the velocity of light, because at this velocity its mass and so inertia becomes infinite. The neutrino, however, is subject neither to gravitational nor to electro-magnetic fields, so that it need not be bound by this speed limit and may have its own, different time. It might be able to travel faster than light, which would make it relativistically recede in our time scale.

. . . From our earlier analysis of mental entities, it appears that they have no definite locus in so-called "physical", or, better, gravi-electromagnetic, space, in which respect they resemble a neutrino or, for that matter, a fast electron. This already suggests a special kind of mental space governed by different laws, which is further corroborated by the parapsychological experiments made at Duke University and elsewhere . . . It seems . . . that this kind of perception involves a mental interaction, which is subject to laws of its own, defining a different type of space-time.[18]

Firsoff's "mindon," is however, a rather primitive model marred by that atomistic interpretation of mental events which psychology is at long last beginning to outgrow. A more sophisticated approach has been suggested by Sir Cyril Burt, whose "psychons"* have configurational rather than particle character, but he did not elaborate on it in detail. The most recent attempts to provide a link between the psi function of quantum mechanics and the psi phenomena of parapsychology were made by the physiologist Sir John Eccles and the mathematician Adrian Dobbs. But they require a preliminary excursion to even wilder shores of modern physics than we have glimpsed so far.

* The term psychon was originally suggested by Whately Carington.

6

In 1931, Paul Adrian Maurice Dirac of Cambridge proposed a theory which would have been rejected as outright crankish if its author had not been one of the outstanding physicists of his time, whose greatest previous achievement (for which he got the Nobel Prize in 1933) had been the unification of Einstein's theory of relativity and Schrödinger's wave mechanics. However, the unified theory ran into new difficulties, which Dirac sought to overcome by postulating that space was not really empty, but filled by a bottomless sea of electrons with *negative mass* (and consequently *negative energy*). Negative mass is of course beyond human imagination; if anything can be said of a particle of this kind it is that if you try to push it forward, it will move backward, and if you blow at it, it will be sucked into your lungs. Since, according to the hypothesis, all available locations in space are uniformly filled with minus-energy electrons, they do not interact, and do not manifest their existence. However, occasionally a high-energy cosmic ray may hit one of these ghost-electrons and impart its own energy to it. As a result, the ghost electron will leap out of the sea, as it were, and become transformed into a normal electron with positive energy and mass. But there is now a "hole", or bubble, left in the sea where the electron had been. This hole will be a negation of negative mass: it will have positive mass. But it will be also a negation of the former occupant's negative electric charge: it will have positive charge. The hole in the cosmic ocean would in fact be, Dirac predicted in 1931, "a new kind of particle unknown to experimental physics, having the same mass as and opposite charge to an electron. We may call such a particle an anti-electron."

But the anti-electron, he further predicted, would be short-lived. Very soon a normal electron would be attracted by the "hole", fall into it, and the two particles would annihilate each other, de-materialising in a flash of high-energy rays.

The theory sounded so wild that Niels Bohr wrote a spoof on it called "How to Catch Elephants". With the school-boy humour which seems to be a characteristic of great physicists, he proposed that big-game hunters should erect at a watering spot frequented by elephants a large poster which briefly summarises Dirac's theory. "When the elephant, who is a proverbially wise animal, comes to have a drink of water, and reads the text on the poster, it will become spellbound for several minutes." Profiting from its trance-like state, the hunter will slip out from his hiding place, tie the elephant's legs with solid ropes, and ship him to the zoo in Copenhagen.*

And yet . . . one year after the publication of Dirac's paper, Carl D. Anderson, working at the California Institute of Technology, was studying the tracks of cosmic-ray electrons in the bubble-chamber, and found that when passing through a strong magnetic field some of them were deflected in a direction opposite to that which normal electrons with a negative charge should follow. Anderson concluded that his weird particles must be positively charged electrons, and called them positrons. They were in fact the "anti-electrons" or "holes" predicted in Dirac's paper—which Anderson had never read.

* I owe this story to George Gamow,[19] and may as well quote here another of Gamow's anecdotes:

"Another example of Dirac's acute observation has a literary flavour. His friend Peter Kapitza, the Russian physicist, gave him an English translation of Dostoyevsky's *Crime and Punishment*.

"'Well, how do you like it?' asked Kapitza when Dirac returned the book.

"'It is nice,' said Dirac, 'but in one of the chapters the author made a mistake. He describes the sun as rising twice on the same day.' This was his one and only comment on Dostoyevsky's novel."[20]

Since the discovery of the anti-electron, physicists have found—or produced in their laboratories—anti-particles corresponding to every known particle. The fifty particles known today and their fifty "antis" are in every respect alike, except that they have opposite electric charges, magnetic moments and opposite "spin" and "strangeness".* But anti-particles are, under normal conditions, very rare: they are either produced by radiation from outer space or by bombarding matter with extremely powerful projectiles; and they are, as already said, very short-lived, because whenever an anti-particle meets its terrestrial *alter ego,* or *Doppelgänger,* they annihilate each other. However, it is considered quite possible that other galaxies are composed of anti-particles, combining into anti-matter; and furthermore, that some spectacular celestial events, such as super-novae or powerful invisible X-ray sources, originated in the collision and mutual annihilation of clouds of matter and anti-matter. These apocalyptic perspectives have become a favourite subject of science-fiction writers—and have also inspired some more quantum poetry. In 1956, Edward Teller (the "father of the hydrogen bomb") gave a lecture in which he enlarged on the explosive consequences of matter getting into contact with anti-matter. A Californian physicist, Harold P. Furth, thereupon wrote a poem which the *New Yorker* printed in November 1956:[21]

> Well up beyond the tropostrata
> There is a region stark and stellar
> Where, on a streak of anti-matter,
> Lived Dr. Edward Anti-Teller.

> Remote from Fusion's origin,
> He lived unguessed and unawares
> With all his anti-kith and kin,
> And kept macassars on his chairs.

* In kindness to the reader I shall not attempt to explain these terms.

One morning, idling by the sea,
He spied a tin of monstrous girth
That bore three letters: A.E.C.*
Out stepped a visitor from Earth.

Then, shouting gladly o'er the sands,
Met two who in their alien ways
Were like lentils. Their right hands
Clasped, and the rest was gamma rays.

7

Yet the theory of an ocean of particles of negative mass, though sufficiently striking to mesmerise an elephant, was regarded with distaste by many physicists. Not because it sounded fantastic; but because it could neither be verified nor refuted by any conceivable method; and it had a suspicious affinity with the nineteenth-century ether. The anti-particles were accepted facts, but physicists were looking for a more elegant theory to account for their behaviour.

One such theory was suggested in 1949 by Richard Phillipps Feynman, also of the California Institute of Technology. He proposed that the positron is nothing but an electron which, for a while, is *moving backwards in time*, and that the same explanation holds for other anti-particles. On the so-called Feynman diagrams, which soon became household articles to physicists, one axis represents time, the other space; particles can move forward and backward in time, and a positron travelling, like all of us, into the future behaves exactly as would an electron travelling momentarily into the past. The time reversals postulated by Feynman are short-lived, because in our

* Atomic Energy Commission.

world anti-particles are short-lived; whether in a galaxy consisting of anti-matter time would permanently flow backward relative to ours is a matter of speculation. But as far as terrestrial physics goes, Feynman's concept of time-reversal proved so productive that in 1953 he received the Albert Einstein Medal and in 1965 the Nobel Prize. The philosopher of science, Hans Reichenbach, wrote that Feynman's theory represented "the most serious blow the concept of time has ever received in physics".[22]

8

Yet the history of science has shown over and over again that the fact that a theory "works" and produces tangible results does not prove that the underlying assumptions are correct; and Feynman's theory presents formidable logical difficulties, even by the permissive standards of modern micro-physics.* Among various attempts to overcome them is the hypothesis, already mentioned, by Adrian Dobbs,† which introduces two time dimensions, instead of one. A five-dimensional universe with three spatial and two temporal dimensions had already been proposed by Eddington and others; but Dobbs' theory contains refinements which take into account the unpredictability and indeterminacy of the future in quantum physics. Accordingly, the arrow of time, progressing along

* See, for instance, G. J. Whitrow's criticism in *The Voices of Time*, ed. J. T. Fraser, London, 1968.
† Adrian Dobbs, who died of an accident while this essay was being written, was a brilliant Cambridge mathematician and physicist engaged in top secret work related to national defence. This was disclosed in a moving obituary by Professor C. D. Broad in the *Journal of the Society for Psychical Research*, December, 1970.

the second time dimension, moves through a probabilistic, instead of a deterministic, world; and it resembles less an arrow than a wave front. However, the main interest of Dobbs' hypothesis lies in his attempt to provide a physicalistic explanation of telepathy and precognition, more sophisticated than any offered before. So sophisticated in fact that it is almost impossible to understand without some working knowledge of quantum theory.

The gist, however, regarding precognition is that the anticipation of future events follows the second time dimension, where "objective probabilities" play the same part as causal relations in classical physics. In Dobbs' own words he proposes "a second time dimension in which the objective probabilities of future outcomes are contained as compresent dispositional factors, which incline or predispose the future to occur in certain specific ways".[23] This has the initial advantage of getting round the old logical paradox that foreknowledge of a future event would imply the possibility of interfering with that event and thus nullifying the foreknowledge.

Dobbs uses the term "pre-cast" instead of "precognition", to indicate that it refers not to prophecy, but to the perception of the probabilistic factors in a system which predispose it towards a given future state. But these pre-casts are not based on guesswork, nor on rational inferences, since the "dispositional factors" of the system cannot be observed or deduced. Information about them is conveyed to the subject by hypothetical messengers which Dobbs calls "psitrons" and which operate in his second time dimension. They are particles with rather startling attributes, but not much more startling than Pauli's neutrino, Dirac's minus-mass electrons, or Feynman's electrons travelling back in time—each of which brought in a Nobel Prize. Dobbs' concept of the psitron is, in fact, the joint product of current trends in quantum theory and brain research. It has *imaginary* mass (in the mathematical sense)* and thus, according to Relativity Theory, can travel faster than light indefinitely, without loss of (imaginary) momentum.

In modern quantum theory processes involving negative or imaginary mass are all in a day's work, so to speak. Professor Margenau of Yale University has given us a picturesque description of this state of affairs:

> At the forefront of current physical research, we find it necessary to invoke the existence of "virtual processes" confined to extremely short durations. For a very short time, every physical process can proceed in ways which defy the laws of nature known today, always hiding itself under the cloak of the principle of uncertainty. When any physical process first starts, it sends out "feelers" in all directions, feelers in which time may be reversed, normal rules are violated, and unexpected things may happen. These virtual processes then die out and after a certain time matters settle down again[24] [compressed].

Professor Bohm of Birkbeck College, University of London, emphasises the same point in his book *Quantum Theory*:

> The preceding description [of certain quantum phenomena] involves the replacement of the classical notion that a system moves along some definite path, by the idea that under the influence of the perturbing potential the system tends to make transitions in all directions at once. Only certain types of transitions can, however, proceed indefinitely in the same

* Imaginary numbers have *negative squares*, although by definition the square of any natural number, whether negative or positive, must be positive ("minus times minus makes plus"). But they are useful tools in quantum physics, where they are equivalent to introducing an added dimension besides ordinary energy, mass or time.

direction, namely those . . . called *real* transitions to distinguish them from the so-called *virtual* transitions which do not conserve energy, and which must therefore reverse before they have gone too far. This terminology is unfortunate, because it implies that virtual transitions have no real effects. On the contrary they are often of the greatest importance, for a great many physical processes are the result of the so-called *virtual* transitions.[25]

In his paper, Dobbs quotes this passage, and comments:

I have quoted this passage at length because the quantum theory of virtual transitions is closely related to the notion I have been suggesting, of an *actual* state of an entity . . . being surrounded in imaginary time with an array of objective probabilities, which are not necessarily actualised, but nonetheless influence the actual course of events... As Bohm says, we have to consider the system as, so to speak, trying out tentatively all the possible potentialities out of which one actuality emerges. Now we can picture these virtual potentialities or probability amplitudes as a swarm of particles of imaginary mass, interacting together like a frictionless gas. . . .[26]

This swarm, or cloud, or "patterned set" of psitrons of imaginary mass, impinging on neurons in the percipient's brain, which are in a particularly receptive condition, would transmit not only information about the *actual* state of the system that emits them but also "pre-casts" of its inherently probable future state, which are already reflected in the "feelers in all directions" which it sends out. Thus the psitrons, Dobbs says, would play an analogous part to that of photons in ordinary vision—except that the psitrons would act directly on the brain, instead of the eye; that they have *imaginary* rest-mass, while the photon's rest-mass is zero; and that they carry information on both *actual* and *virtual* processes, the latter "precasting" the immediate future. If the reader finds much of this obscure, he must seek comfort in the thought that obscurity is, so to speak, built into quantum physics like the holes into a Gruyère cheese.

On the crucial question, how the hypothetical psitrons could convey information direct to the percipient's brain, short-circuiting, as it were, the sensory apparatus, Dobbs resorted to a theory advanced some years ago by Sir John Eccles. This eminent physiologist received the 1963 Nobel Prize for his pioneering work on the transmisson of nerve-impulses across the synaptic junctions between brain-cells. In the last chapter of his textbook on *The Neurophysiological Basis of Mind* Eccles launched what he called a "Hypothesis of the mode of operation of 'Will' on the cerebral cortex". The hypothesis is not concerned with precognition, but what it says about the interaction of mind and matter is pertinent to the subject, and I shall have to quote from it at some length.

It is a psychological fact that we believe we have ability to control or modify our actions by the exercise of "will", and in practical life all sane men assume that they have this ability. By stimulation of the motor-cortex [of the exposed brain of patients undergoing a brain operation] it is possible to evoke complex motor acts in a conscious human subject. The subject reports that the experience is quite different from that occurring when he "willed" a movement ... In one case there was the experience of having "willed" an action, which was missing in the other.*

* For a more detailed account of these experiments, first reported by Wilder Penfield, see *The Ghost in the Machine*, pp. 203–4.

It is not here contended that all action is "willed". There can be no doubt that a great part of the skilled activity devolving from the cerebral cortex is stereotyped and automatic, and may be likened to the control of breathing by the respiratory centres. But it is contended that it is possible voluntarily to assume control of such actions, even of the most trivial kind, just as we may within limits exercise voluntary control over our breathing. . . .

An important neurophysiological problem arises as soon as we attempt to consider in detail the events that would occur in the cerebral cortex when, by the exercise of "will", there is some change in response to a given situation. . . .[27]

Eccles then proceeds to work out a concise theory of how a minute "will-influence", affecting *a single neuron* in the cortex, could trigger off very considerable changes in brain activity. The trigger-action would affect neurons which are "critically poised", as he puts it, i.e. in unstable equilibrium, just below the threshold of discharging a nerve impulse.* In view of the fact that there are some forty

---

* As a matter of curiosity I may be permitted to mention here that in an earlier book—*The Yogi and the Commissar*, published in 1943—I made a suggestion which seems in some respects to anticipate Eccles' theory of the "will" acting on "critically poised" brain cells, thus giving rise to conscious actions:

"Volition may be regarded as the psychological aspect or projection of the interplay of impulses and inhibitions. If this interplay takes place on the conscious level it is experienced as a not enforced, not inevitable process of choice. This subjective experience of freedom is the stronger the closer the process to the focus of attention. Actions resulting from processes on the pre-conscious fringes are experienced as 'absent-minded' semi-automatic doings, and from extra-conscious processes as fully automatic.

"The experience of freedom resulting from processes in the focus of attention is probably synonymous with consciousness itself. Its essential characteristic is that the process is experienced as working from inside outwards instead of from outwards in; it seems deter-

thousand neurons packed together per square millimetre (approximately $\frac{1}{700}$ square inch) of the cerebral cortex, and that each neuron has several hundred synaptic connections with other neurons, we have here a network of such density and complexity that

> in the active cerebral cortex within twenty milliseconds, the pattern of discharge of even hundreds of thousands of neurons would be modified as a result of an "influence" that initially caused the discharge of merely one neuron . . .
>
> Thus, the neurophysiological hypothesis is that the "will" modifies the spatio-temporal activity of the neuronal network by exerting spatio-temporal "fields of influence" that become affected through this unique detector function of the active cerebral cortex.[30]

Eccles is a determined opponent of the positivist argument that while "brain" is a reality, "mind" is a fiction—a ghost in the machine:

> It will be objected [he writes] that the essence of the hypothesis is that mind produces changes in the matter-energy system of the brain and hence must be itself in that system . . . But this deduction is merely based on the present hypotheses of physics. Since these postulated "mind-influences" have not been detected by any existing physical instrument, they have necessarily been neglected in constructing the hypotheses of physics . . . It is at least claimed that the active cerebral cortex could be a detector of

mined from the subject's core and not by outward environment. On the psychological plane the experience of freedom is as much a given datum or 'reality' as are sense perceptions or the feeling of pain . . .[28] Incidentally, the state of 'precarious balance' which characterises the emergence of experienced freedom is also characteristic of the original instability of organic molecules and other emergent biological levels."[29]

such "influences", even if they existed at any intensity below that detectable by physical instruments. It would appear that it is the sort of machine a "ghost" could operate.[31]

So far Eccles has been discussing the action of individual minds on their "own" brains. In the concluding sections of his book, however, he lifts this restriction and includes ESP and PK into the theory. He accepts the experiments of Rhine, Thouless, Soal, etc. as evidence for a generalised "two-way traffic" between mind and matter, and for a direct traffic between mind and mind. He believes that ESP and PK are weak and irregular manifestations of the *same* principle which allows an individual's mental volition to influence his own material brain, and the material brain to give rise to conscious experiences. He also reminds us of an unduly neglected hypothesis, which Eddington formulated in 1939, of a "correlated behaviour of the individual particles of matter, which he assumed to occur for matter in liaison with mind. The behaviour of such matter would stand in sharp contrast to the un-correlated or random behaviour of particles that is postulated in physics".[32]

Let us now return to Dobbs. Eccles seems to have deliberately abstained from giving any indication of the supposed nature of those "influences" or "influence-fields" which are meant to serve as vehicles for the traffic between matter and mind, or mind and mind. Dobbs proposed to provide such a carrier by the psitron which, when it impinges on the "critically poised" neurons in the brain, can trigger off "a cascade or chain reaction" of neural events.

Although Dobbs' hypothesis includes telepathy, clairvoyance and precognition, it says nothing about the problem of how mind and brain interact in one and the same ordinary person—which was Eccles' starting point.

Dobbs is not directly concerned with the mind-body problem; he takes it for granted that certain processes in the brain give rise "to certain states of awareness"— and that applies regardless of whether the brain processes in question were induced by extra-sensory, or common sensory, perception. The distance in space which the psitron has to travel is irrelevant—as it is irrelevant to neutrinos.

Thus we arrive at the paradoxical conclusion that physicalistic theories such as Adrian Dobbs', however ingenious, may explain the "extra" in extra-sensory perception, but leave the basic mystery of ordinary, sensory perception where it was before. But at least these theories, based on assumptions which sound weird but hardly more weird than those of modern physics, go a long way towards removing the aura of superstition from the "extra" in extra-sensory perception. The odour of the alchemist's kitchen is replaced by the smell of quark in the laboratory. The rapprochement between the conceptual world of parapsychology and that of modern physics is an important step towards the demolition of the greatest superstition of our age—the materialistic clock-work universe of early-nineteenth-century physics. "To assert that there is *only matter* and no mind", Firsoff wrote, "is the most illogical of propositions, quite apart from the findings of modern physics, which show that there is no matter in the traditional meaning of the term."[33] Or, once more, Sir Cyril Burt (who has an irresistible effect on writers suffering from "Quoter's Itch"):

And so we arrive at the current conception of the brain as a kind of computer, and of human beings as mere conscious automata. "If you think we are wax-works," said Tweedledum to Alice, "you ought to pay." And contemporary psychology has had to pay a heavy price for adhering to this mechanistic doctrine.

77

It makes nonsense, not only of parapsychology, but (as practical psychologists have long been protesting) of every branch of applied psychology—criminology, psychotherapy, educational and vocational guidance, and of all moral or aesthetic aspirations and values. As a theory of the relation of body and mind, [materialism] rests on a glaring inconsistency ... In a purely mechanical world of cause and effect, ruled by the law of the conservation of energy, no "phenomenon" ... could possibly appear without some appropriate cause. Within the nervous system, therefore, so [it was] ... suggested, energy must in some inexplicable fashion be "transformed" into consciousness. The chemistry of the brain must "generate" it, much as the liver generates bile. How the motions of material particles could possibly "generate" this "insubstantial pageant" remained a mystery. Any such process would obviously be, not physical, but psychophysical; so that the perfection of a purely physical universe was already rudely violated.[34]

9

At the beginning of this essay I suggested that the seemingly fantastic propositions of parapsychology appear less preposterous in the light of the truly fantastic concepts of modern physics. My purpose in describing Dobbs' theory* in the context of quantum mechanics was merely to illustrate this point—without any claim that the theory

---

* At the end of Dobbs' main paper[35] he proposes an experimental programme, including a certain type of EEG test during ESP experiments, which, he maintained, would confirm or refute his theory. It is to be hoped that in spite of his untimely death, the experiments will be made (although for reasons too technical to explain, I would predict a negative result).

is correct, or even on the right lines; I could have cited other hypotheses to make the same point. Physicists are not shy, as we saw, of producing *ad hoc* hypotheses—or speculations—to accommodate newly discovered phenomena which do not fit into the existing framework. The Greeks knew the electrical properties of amber—or *elektron*—but were not interested. For some two thousand years nobody was interested. When, in the seventeenth century, experimenting with electricity became fashionable, previously undreamt-of phenomena were discovered, and scientists vied in proposing hypotheses to account for them—postulating effluvia, liquid fires, currents, fields, without turning a hair. Magnetism and gravity had a similar history: when Kepler suggested that the tides are due to attractive forces emanating from the moon, Galileo shrugged the idea off as an "occult fancy" because it involved action-at-a-distance and thus contradicted the "laws of nature"; but that did not deter Newton from postulating universal gravity. *"Hypothesis non fingo"* is perhaps the most shocking piece of hypocrisy ever uttered by a great scientist.

This does not mean that hypothesis-making is a free-for-all. To produce live rabbits out of a hat needs a skilled magician. Quantum physics may be mad, but it has method, and it works. I talked earlier on of a *negative* rapprochement between quantum physics and ESP, in so far as the surrealistic concepts of the former make it easier to suspend disbelief in the latter; if the former is permitted to violate the "laws of nature" as they were understood by classical physics a century ago, the latter may claim the same right. But to stress the point once more, this is merely a negative agreement, a shared disregard for ancient taboos, for a mechanistic world-view which has become an anachronism.

That is all to the good. There are, however, phenomena in parapsychology which no physicist, however open-minded, can willingly accept on face value: I mean PK—psychokinesis.

The "extra" bit in extra-sensory *perception* may quite possibly become in the not too distant future amenable to theoretical treatment in terms of quantum physics enriched by new "fields" added to the existing ones, and new types of "interactions" added to the existing repertory of four.* But such optimism seems less justified when it comes to psychokinesis. Dobbs is silent about it, so is Margenau, and—within my limited knowledge of parapsychological literature—I am unaware of any serious attempt at a physicalistic explanation of how a mental effort could influence the motions of rolling dice. The reason is simple: ESP and PK are operating in different dimensions; and just as the rigid mechanical laws of the macroscopic world do not apply to micro-physics, so the freedom enjoyed in the realm of micro-physics does not apply to the macroscopic level. An atom is "free" to do this or that within Heisenberg's indeterminacy relation, and all our statements about it refer to probabilities, not to certainties. But according to the law of large numbers, in a macroscopic body of trillions of atoms, the deviations cancel out, the sum of probabilities results in practical certainty, and the old taboos retain their validity.† Thus when an ESP message in the shape of mindons, psitrons or what-have-you impinges on a "critically poised" neuron, it operates on the quantum indeterminacy level and can do wonders, so to speak. But this process is

---

* Contemporary physics knows four types of interaction: the "strong" and "weak" nuclear interactions; the electro-magnetic and the gravitational. Each obeys its own set of laws.

† To illustrate this point, the uncertainty attaching to the whereabouts of a single electron in a hydrogen atom is "smeared" over the whole length of its "planetary orbit". But the velocity of a small buckshot is uncertain only within about twelve inches per century, and the uncertainty of its position is only the size of the diameter of the atomic nucleus.[36]

not reversible. You cannot influence the progress of a macroscopic body like a rolling die, by micro-physical particles or wavicles of imaginary mass. Thus the law of large numbers, which lends such authority to the evidence for ESP, is at the same time the main obstacle to any physicalistic explanation of PK.*

But this does not mean that the evidential value of the macroscopic PK experiments, by Rhine and others, is to be disregarded. It only means that, though we have to accept the evidence, we have to renounce any reasonable hope of a physical explanation, even in terms of the most advanced and permissive quantum mechanics.

The same dilemma confronts us as we turn to a type of phenomenon which has puzzled man since the dawn of mythology: the disruption of the humdrum chains of causal events by coincidences of an improbable nature, which are not causally related yet appear highly significant. Any theory which attempts to take such phenomena seriously must necessarily involve an even more radical break with our traditional categories of thought than the pronunciamentos of Heisenberg, Dirac or Feynman. It is certainly no coincidence that it was Wolfgang Pauli— father of the neutrino and of the "Pauli Principle", a cornerstone of modern physics—who outlined such a theory, in collaboration with C. G. Jung.

The Jung–Pauli theory of "Synchronicity", conceived by a physicist and a psychologist, both eminent in their fields, represents perhaps the most radical departure from the world-view of mechanistic science in our time. Yet they had a precursor, whose ideas had a considerable influence on Jung: the Austrian biologist Paul Kammerer, a wild genius who committed suicide in 1926, at the age of forty-five.

---

* The importance of Helmut Schmidt's revolutionary experiments with electronic equipment, discussed earlier on, lies precisely in the fact that they operate on the quantum level. But you cannot extrapolate from there to dice.

3
Seriality and Synchronicity

I

Kammerer was a Lamarckian: he believed in the "inheritance of acquired characteristics"—that the skills and improvements in physique acquired by the parents are to some extent inherited by their offspring. As against this, the orthodox neo-Darwinian theory holds that acquired characteristics do not affect the genes, carriers of the hereditary blueprint; evolution is the outcome of random mutations in the genetic material, retained by natural selection. The Lamarckian view is philosophically more attractive, because it regards evolution as the cumulative effect of the virtues and strivings of successive generations, whereas in the Darwinian view these efforts are wasted, each generation must start from scratch, as it were, and evolution is the result of blind chance and selective pressures. But the Lamarckians have never been able to produce experimental evidence of the inheritance of acquired characteristics; Lamarckism went out of fashion at the beginning of the century and came to be regarded as a heresy. Kammerer was the last Lamarckian of European fame; he spent most of his life trying to demonstrate the inheritance of acquired characters in reptiles, amphibians and even in sea-squirts. But his experimental animals perished in the First World War; and his last preserved specimen, a so-called "midwife toad" (*Alytes obstetricans*) was found to have been tampered with to fake the evidence. A few weeks after this disclosure, his reputation ruined, Kammerer shot himself on an Austrian mountain.

I have for many years been fascinated by this extraordinary personality, and have recently written his biography* which, I believe, contains strong evidence indicating that the forgery was committed, without his knowledge, by a different person. In the present context, however, we are concerned not with Kammerer's Lamarckian views (though I shall briefly return to them later on), but with a second heresy to which he was committed: his belief in the significance of apparent coincidences. He published his theory on the subject in 1919, in a remarkable work, *Das Gesetz der Serie*—the law of seriality; no English translation exists to date. I have given a summary of the book in Appendix I of *The Case of the Midwife Toad*, and must apologise for repeating some passages from it.

Kammerer kept a log-book of coincidences from the age of twenty to forty. He was not the only one to indulge in this secret vice; Jung, for instance, did the same. "I have often come up against the phenomena in question", Jung wrote, "and could convince myself how much these inner experiences meant to my patients. In most cases they were things which people do not talk about for fear of exposing themselves to thoughtless ridicule. I was amazed to see how many people have had experiences of this kind, and how carefully the secret was guarded."[1]

Kammerer's book contains a hundred samples of coincidences. For instance:

(7) On September 18, 1916, my wife, while waiting for her turn in the consulting rooms of Prof. Dr. J. v. H., reads the magazine *Die Kunst*; she is impressed by some reproductions of pictures by a painter named

* *The Case of the Midwife Toad* (London, 1971, New York 1972).

Schwalbach, and makes a mental note to remember his name because she would like to see the originals. At that moment the door opens and the receptionist calls out to the patients: "Is Frau Schwalbach here? She is wanted on the telephone."[2]

(22) On July 28, 1915, I experienced the following progressive series: (a) my wife was reading about "Mrs. Rohan", a character in the novel *Michael* by Hermann Bang; in the tramway she saw a man who looked like her friend, Prince Josef Rohan; in the evening Prince Rohan dropped in on us. (b) In the tram she overheard somebody asking the pseudo-Rohan whether he knew the village of Weissenbach on Lake Attersee, and whether it would be a pleasant place for a holiday. When she got out of the tram, she went to a delicatessen shop on the Naschmarkt, where the attendant asked her whether she happened to know Weissenbach on Lake Attersee—he had to make a delivery by mail and did not know the correct postal address.[3]

Most of his other examples are even more trivial;* thus he records that on November 4, 1910, his brother-in-law went to a concert where he had seat No. 9 and cloakroom ticket No. 9; the next day, at another concert, he had seat No. 21 and cloakroom ticket No. 21. Kammerer calls this a "series of the second order" because the same type of coincidence occurred on two successive days, and comments: "We shall soon see that such clusterings of series of the first order into series of the second or *n*th order are common, almost regular occurrences."[4]

It is indeed commonly believed that coincidences tend to come in series—gamblers have "lucky days", and

* For this reason I have quoted the same two samples as in *The Case of the Midwife Toad.*

vice versa, "it never rains but it pours". Hence the title of the book, *Das Gesetz der Serie*. He defines a *Serie* as "a lawful recurrence of the same or similar things and events —a recurrence, or clustering, in time or space whereby the individual members in the sequence—as far as can be ascertained by careful analysis—are not connected by the same active cause".[5]

The expression "*lawful* recurrence" may give the impression that the series is governed by causal laws. But Kammerer's purpose is to prove just the opposite— that coincidences, whether they come singly or in series, are manifestations of a universal principle in nature which operates *independently from physical causation*. The "laws of Seriality" are, in Kammerer's view, as fundamental as those of physics, but as yet unexplored. Moreover, single coincidences are merely tips of the iceberg which happened to catch our eye, because in our traditional ways we tend to ignore the ubiquitous manifestations of Seriality.

The first half of Kammerer's book is devoted to the classification of coincidental series, which he undertook with the meticulousness of a zoologist devoted to taxonomy. There is a *typology* of non-causal concurrences related to numbers, names, situations, etc. After this comes a chapter on the *morphology* of Series, which are classified according to their "*order*" (the number of successive coincidences), their *power* (number of parallel coincidences) and their *parameters* (number of shared attributes).

Kammerer spent hours sitting on benches in various public parks, noting down the numbers of people that strolled by in both directions, classifying them by sex, age, dress, whether they carried umbrellas or parcels. He did the same on his long tram journeys from suburb to laboratory. Then he analysed his tables and found that on every parameter they showed the typical clustering phenomena familiar to statisticians, gamblers and insurance companies. He made the necessary allowances for such causal factors as rush-hour, weather, etc.[6]

At the end of this classificatory part of the book Kammerer concluded:

So far we have been concerned with the factual manifestations of recurrent series, without attempting an explanation. We have found that the recurrence of identical or similar data in contiguous areas of space or time is a simple empirical fact which has to be accepted and which cannot be explained by coincidence—or rather, which makes coincidence rule to such an extent that the concept of coincidence itself is negated.[7]

In the second, theoretical part of the book, Kammerer develops his central idea that coexistent with causality there is an a-causal principle active in the universe, which tends towards unity. In some respects it is comparable to universal gravity—which, to the physicist, is also still a mystery; but unlike gravity which acts on all *mass* indiscriminately, this force acts selectively on *form and function* to bring similar configurations together in space and time; it correlates by *affinity*. By which means this a-causal agency intrudes into the causal order of things— both in dramatic and trivial ways—we cannot tell, since it functions *ex hypothesi*, outside the known laws of physics. In space it produces concurrent events related by affinity; in time similarly related series. "We thus arrive at the image of a world-mosaic or cosmic kaleidoscope, which, in spite of constant shufflings and rearrangements, also takes care of bringing like and like together."[8]

Kammerer was particularly interested in temporal Series of recurrent events; these he regarded as cyclic processes which propagate themselves like waves along the time-axis of the space-time continuum. But we are aware only of the crests of the waves, which appear to us as isolated coincidences, while the troughs remain unnoticed. (He thus reverses the sceptic's argument that out of the multitude of random events we only pick those which are significant.) The cycles may be caused either by causal factors (i.e. planetary motion) or patterned by Seriality—as the lucky runs of gamblers. He devotes a chapter to previous theories of periodicity, from the Pythagoreans' magic seven to Goethe's "revolving circles of good and bad days", up to Freud—who believed in cycles of twenty-three and twenty-seven days which somehow combine to produce the data of significant events.

At the end of the book Kammerer expresses his belief that Seriality is "ubiquitous and continuous in life, nature and cosmos. It is the umbilical cord that connects thought, feeling, science and art with the womb of the universe which gave birth to them."[9]

Some of the chapters in the book, particularly those dealing with physics, contain naive errors; others show tantalising flashes of intuition. I have compared its effect to that of an Impressionist painting which has to be viewed from a distance; if one puts one's nose into it, the details turn into clumsy blobs. While thus the theoretical part can hardly stand up to critical scrutiny, this first attempt at a systematic classification of coincidental events may find some unexpected applications at some future date. These things happen in science. It may also be the reason why Einstein gave a favourable opinion of the book; he called it "original and by no means absurd".* He may have remembered that the non-

* Quoted by H. Przibram, "*Paul Kammerer als Biologe*", *Monistische Monatshefte*, November, 1926.

Euclidian geometries, invented by earlier mathematicians more or less as a game, provided the basis for his relativistic cosmology.

2

Another great physicist whose thoughts moved in a similar direction was Wolfgang Pauli.

At the end of the 1932 conference on nuclear physics in Copenhagen the participants, as was their custom on these occasions, performed a skit full of that quantum humour of which we have already had a few samples. In that particular year they produced a parody of Goethe's *Faust*, in which Wolfgang Pauli was cast in the role of Mephistopheles; his Gretchen was the neutrino, whose existence Pauli had predicted, but which had not yet been discovered.

MEPHISTOPHELES (to Faust):
Beware, beware, of Reason and of Science
Man's highest powers, unholy in alliance.
You'll let yourself, through dazzling witchcraft yield
To weird temptations of the quantum field.

Enter Gretchen; she sings to Faust. Melody: "Gretchen at the Spinning Wheel" by Schubert.

GRETCHEN:

My rest-mass is zero
My charge is the same
You are my hero
Neutrino's my name.

Well . . . But Pauli really was a kind of Mephisto

among the sorcerers of Copenhagen. Years earlier he had produced, by a brilliant sleight of hand, one of the key concepts of modern physics, the Pauli Exclusion Principle, which says, roughly speaking, that only one electron at a time can occupy any "planetary orbit" inside an atom.* The Exclusion Principle was a purely mathematical construct, for which no justification in terms of physical causation could be invoked—except the fact that without it quantum theory made no sense. The Professor of Physics at Yale commented:

> Men in theoretical physics today invoke a principle known as the "Exclusion Principle": it was discovered by Pauli. It is responsible for most of the organising actions that occur in nature. All of these are brought about by the Pauli principle, which is simply a principle of symmetry, a formal mathematical characteristic of the equations which in the end regulate phenomena in nature. Almost miraculously it calls into being what we call exchange forces, the forces which bind atoms into molecules and molecules into crystals. It is responsible for the fact that iron can be magnetised, that matter cannot be squeezed together into an arbitrarily small volume. The impenetrability of matter, its very stability, can be directly traced to the Pauli Exclusion Principle. Now, this principle has no dynamic aspect to it at all. It acts like a force although it is not a force. We cannot speak of it as doing anything by mechanical action. No, it is a very general and elusive thing; a mathematical symmetry imposed upon the basic equations of nature.[10]

Pauli shared Kammerer's and Jung's belief in non-

---

* More precisely: that in a neutral atom no two electrons can have the same set of quantum numbers.

causal, non-physical factors operating in nature. Even the Exclusion Principle "acts like a force although it is not a force". He probably had a more profound insight than his fellow-sorcerers into the limitations of science. When he was fifty, he wrote a penetrating study on the emergence of science from mysticism, as reflected in the ideas of Johannes Kepler—who was both a mystic and the founder of modern astronomy.* The essay is called "The Influence of Archetypal Ideas on the Scientific Theories of Kepler", and originally appeared in a series of monographs published by the Jung Institute in Zürich.[11]

It was a highly unusual enterprise for a modern scientist to engage in this kind of writing, and to have it printed in a psychological journal. Towards the end of his essay Pauli says: "Today we have the natural sciences, but no longer a philosophy of science. Since the discovery of the elementary quantum, physics was obliged to renounce its proud claim to be able to understand in principle the *whole* of the world. But this predicament may contain the seed of further developments which will correct the previous one-sided orientation and will move towards a unitary world-view in which science is only a part in the whole."[12]

This kind of philosophical doubt about "the meaning of it all" is not unusual among scientists when they get over fifty. One might almost call it the rule. Hence the galaxy of FRSs and Nobel Laureates in the Society for Psychical Research's role of honour. But Pauli went further than devising physicalistic theories to explain ESP in causal terms. He felt that this was hopeless, and that it was preferable and more honest to accept that parapsychological phenomena, including apparent coin-

* Cf. my biography of Kepler in *The Sleepwalkers* and the analysis, which is very close to Pauli's, of his intellectual development in my article on Kepler in the *Encyclopaedia of Philosophy*.

cidences, were the visible traces of untraceable a-causal principles in the universe. This provided the basis for his collaboration with Jung.

3

Jung used Pauli, so to speak, as a tutor in modern physics. Jung had experimented in parapsychology and spiritualism from his early days as a student of medicine, to the end of his life. He refused "to commit the fashionable stupidity of regarding everything I cannot explain as a fraud".[13] In his early twenties he organised regular spiritualistic séances; in the course of one of these "a heavy walnut table, an old heirloom, split with a loud report, and soon afterwards a bread-knife in a drawer inexplicably snapped into four parts, again with a sound like a pistol shot. The four pieces of the knife are still in the possession of the Jung family."[14]

In his memoirs Jung relates a famous episode which took place when, in 1909, he visited Freud in Vienna, during the honeymoon of their collaboration (the break was to come three years later). Jung wanted to know Freud's opinion on ESP. Freud, at that time, rejected it, although in later years he changed his mind. Jung narrates:

While Freud was going on this way, I had a curious sensation. It was as if my diaphragm was made of iron and was becoming red-hot—a glowing vault. And at that moment there was such a loud report in the bookcase, which stood right next to us, that we both started up in alarm, fearing the thing was going to topple over us. I said to Freud: "There, that is an example of a so-called catalytic exteriorisation phenomenon."

"Oh come," he exclaimed. "That is sheer bosh."

"It is not," I replied. "You are mistaken, Herr Professor. And to prove my point I now predict that in a moment there will be another loud report!" Sure enough, no sooner had I said the words than the same detonation went off in the bookcase.

To this day I do not know what gave me this certainty. But I knew beyond all doubt that the report would come again. Freud only stared aghast at me. I do not know what was in his mind, or what his look meant. In any case, this incident aroused his mistrust of me, and I had the feeling that I had done something against him. I never afterwards discussed the incident with him.[15]

Though he experimented with mediums, Jung initially drew the line at ghosts. In a lecture to the English Society for Psychical Research in 1919 he explained apparitions and apparent materialisations as "unconscious projections" or "exteriorisations":

I for one am certainly convinced that they are exteriorisations. I have repeatedly observed the telepathic effects of unconscious complexes, and also a number of parapsychic phenomena, but in all this I see no proof whatever of the existence of real spirits, and until such proof is forthcoming I must regard this whole territory as an appendix of psychology.[16]

How an "exteriorisation" of an emotional state could produce the detonations in Freud's bookcase remained for the time being an unresolved question. But the next year Jung met a real ghost—in England, of course. He described the event in a little-known anthology.[17] He spent several weekends in a country house in Buckinghamshire which a friend had recently rented. During several nights he heard all sorts of noises—the dripping of water, rustlings, knockings, which increased in intensity until, during the fifth weekend, he thought somebody outside was knocking at the wall with a sledge-hammer. "I had the feeling of a close presence. I opened my eyes with an effort. Then I saw lying next to my head on the pillow, the head of an old woman whose right eye, wide open, was staring at me. The left half of her face, including the eye, was missing. I leapt out of bed and lit a candle." Thereupon the head vanished. Later on, Jung and his host discovered that the whole village knew the house was haunted. It was torn down soon after.

Jung seemed to have been pursued by this kind of experience all his life. Some of his patients, too, became susceptible to them. A typical case is the following:

A young woman I was treating had, at a critical moment, a dream in which she was given a golden scarab. While she was telling me this dream I sat with my back to the closed window. Suddenly I heard a noise behind me, like a gentle tapping. I turned round and saw a flying insect knocking against the window-pane from outside. I opened the window and caught the creature in the air as it flew in. It was the nearest analogy to a golden scarab that one finds in our latitudes, a scarabaeid beetle, the common rose-chafer (*Cetonia aurata*), which contrary to its usual habits had evidently felt an urge to get into a dark room at this particular moment.[18]

At some point in his life Jung became convinced that such phenomena transcended the realm of "ordinary" ESP and that a more radical approach was needed to find a place for them in our mental outlook. In his lecture to the English SPR in 1919 he had denied the existence of "real spirits" and maintained that "this whole territory was an appendix to psychology". But when the lecture was reprinted in his *Collected Works* in 1947, he appended a footnote to this passage:

After collecting psychological experiences from many people and many countries for fifty years, I no longer feel as certain as I did in 1919, when I wrote this sentence. To put it bluntly, I doubt whether an exclusively psychological approach can do justice to the phenomena in question. Not only the findings of parapsychology, but my own theoretical reflections outlined in *On the Nature of the Psyche*[19] have led me to certain postulates which touch on the realms of nuclear physics and the whole conception of the space-time continuum. This opens up the whole question of the transpsychic reality immediately underlying the psyche.[20]

4

At about the time when this was written Jung was working, in collaboration with Pauli, on his treatise on *Synchronicity: An Acausal Connecting Principle,* which was published together with Pauli's essay on Kepler in one volume. This was evidently meant as a symbolic act: one of the greatest physicists of the century joining forces with one of its greatest psychologists. The result was a stimulating exercise in unorthodox speculation, but at the same time sadly disappointing. It did not amount to a theory in the proper sense, but rather to a universal schema, both very bold and very vague.

Jung's treatise hinges on his concept of "Synchronicity". He defines it as "the simultaneous occurrence of two meaningfully but not causally connected events";[21] or alternatively as "a coincidence in time of two or more causally unrelated events which have the same or similar meaning[22] . . . equal in rank to causality as a principle of explanation".[23] This is an almost verbatim repetition of Kammerer's definition of "Seriality" as "a recurrence of the same or similar things or events in time or space" —events which, as far as can be ascertained, "are not connected by the same acting cause". The main difference appears to be that Kammerer emphasises serial happenings in time (though, of course, he includes contemporaneous coincidences in space), whereas Jung's concept of synchronicity seems to refer only to simultaneous events —although he includes precognitive dreams which occurred sometimes several days before the events. He tried to get around the time paradox by saying that the unconscious mind functions outside of the physical framework of space-time; thus precognitive experiences are "evidently not *synchronous* but are *synchronistic* since they are experienced as psychic images *in the present* as though the objective event already existed".[24] One wonders why Jung created these unnecessary complications by coining a term which implies simultaneity, and then explaining that it does not mean what it means. But this kind of obscurity combined with verbosity runs through much of Jung's writing.

Although Kammerer's "Seriality" and Jung's "Synchronicity" are as similar as a pair of gloves, each fits one hand only. Kammerer confined himself to analogies in naive physical terms, rejecting ESP and mentalistic explanations. Jung went to the opposite extreme and tried to explain all phenomena which could not be accounted for in terms of physical causality, as manifestations of the unconscious mind: "Synchronicity is a phenomenon that seems to be primarily connected with psychic conditions, that is to say with processes in the unconscious."[25] Its deepest strata, according to Jungian terminology, are formed by the "collective unconscious", potentially shared by all members of the race. The "decisive factors" in the collective unconscious are the archetypes which "constitute its structure".[26] They are, as it were, the distilled memories of the human species, but cannot be represented in verbal terms, only in elusive symbols, shared by all mythologies. They also provide "patterns of behaviour"[27] for all human beings in archetypal situations—confrontations with death, danger, love, conflict, etc. In such situations the unconscious archetypes invade consciousness, carrying strong emotions and—owing perhaps to the archetype's indifference to physical space and time—facilitate the occurrence of "synchronistic" events. The appearance of the scarab while the patient was telling her archetypal dream is considered by Jung as an illustration of this nexus. The same applies to the detonations in Freud's bookcase during Jung's visit, indicating the explosive nature of their father-son relationship: "Meaningful coincidences—which are to be distinguished from meaningless chance-groupings—therefore seem to rest on an archetypal foundation. At least all the cases in my experience—and there is a large number of them—show this characteristic."[28]

Elsewhere in the essay he writes:

Synchronistic events rest on the *simultaneous occurrence of two different psychic states*. One of them is the normal, probable state (i.e., the one that is causally explicable), and the other, the critical experience, is the one that cannot be derived causally from the first. In the case of sudden death, the critical experience cannot be recognised immediately as "extra-sensory perception" but can only be verified as such afterwards. . . . In all these cases, whether it is a question of spatial or of temporal ESP, we find a simultaneity of the normal or ordinary state with another state or experience which is not causally derivable from it, and whose objective existence can only be verified afterwards. . . . An unexpected [mental] content which is directly or indirectly connected with some objective external event coincides with the ordinary psychic state: this is what I call synchronicity.[29]

The obscurity of these and similar passages indicates the apparently insurmountable difficulties of breaking away from our ingrained habits of thinking in terms of cause and effect. Kammerer started with an intuitive conviction of the existence of a-causal forces in the universe, and landed up with his spurious physical analogies. Jung, starting from the same premiss as Kammerer, ended up with the confused notion that his archetypes somehow engineered the detonations in the bookcase, or the scarab's appearance at the window. To resolve this paradox he postulated that the archetypes were psycho-physical entities ("psychoids"), whose "trans-psychic reality" may produce not only detonations but also ghosts—see the note revoking his earlier disbelief in the existence of "real spirits".*

In the same breath he wrote: "We must completely give up the idea of the psyche's being somehow connected

* See also the comments of one of his close collaborators, Aniela Jaffé: "The postulate of an imperceivable psychoid background world colours the initial problem of 'ghosts' only to this extent: Jung could no longer maintain with assurance that these apparitions are projections of psychic complexes. Jung expressed himself very cautiously in his Preface to the German edition of Stewart Edward White's *The Unobstructed Universe*:

" 'Although on the one hand our critical arguments throw doubt on every single case [of apparitions], there is on the other hand not a single argument which could disprove the existence of ghosts. In this regard, therefore, we must probably content ourselves with a non liquet.' "[30]

with the brain, and remember instead the 'meaningful' or 'intelligent' behaviour of the lower organisms, which are without a brain. Here we find ourselves much closer to the formal factor which, as I have said, has nothing to do with brain activity." The term "formal factor" refers to a presumed archetypal consciousness in the amoeba; but this could hardly justify the denial of the connection between human consciousness and the human brain. It is painful to watch how a great mind, trying to disentangle himself from the causal chains of materialistic science, gets entangled in its own verbiage.

Kammerer and Jung, in their different ways, fell into the same trap: Whitehead called it "misplaced concreteness". Like theologians who start from the premiss that the mind of God is beyond human understanding and then proceed to explain how the mind of God works, they postulated an a-causal principle, and proceeded to explain it in pseudo-causal terms.

How Pauli reacted to all this we can only guess. He must have realised that Jung's theory of the archetype as a *deus ex machina* was a non-starter, but apart from tutoring Jung in theoretical physics (of which in the end Jung made little use), it seems unlikely that Pauli had much influence on Jung's paper.* Pauli's own essay, turning the mental evolution of Kepler into a paradigm of the limitations of science, is a model of clarity in sharp contrast to Jung's meanderings.† But the comparison is not quite fair because it is, as we have seen, much easier for a modern physicist than for a psychologist to get out

* One wonders whether anybody else had—and whether Jung himself had even read the proofs. If he had, it remains incomprehensible that he did not amend the flat nonsense about there being no connection between mind and brain.

† Pauli's essay is, as we remember, called "The Influence of Archetypal Ideas on the Scientific Theories of Kepler"; but he uses the word "archetypal" in its classic, Platonic meaning (as Kepler himself did), and not in the way Jung abused it.

of the grooves of causality, matter, space-time and other traditional categories of thought. The physicist has been trained to regard the world as experienced by our senses as an illusion—Eddington's shadow-desk, covered by the veil of Maya. But that does not worry him unduly, because he has created a world of his own, described in a language of great beauty and power, the language of mathematical equations, which tells him all he knows, and can ever hope to know, of the universe around him. Bertrand Russell did not mean to be ironical when he wrote: "Physics is mathematical not because we know so much about the physical world, but because we know so little: it is only its mathematical properties that we can discover."

Thus the physicist was able to discard, one by one, all commonsense ideas of what the world is like—without suffering any traumatic shock.* One by one, matter, energy and causality were dethroned; but the physicist was richly compensated by being able to play around with such enticing Gretchens as the neutrino, and with such exhilarating notions as time flowing backward, ghost-particles of negative mass, and atoms of radium spontaneously emitting beta radiation without physical cause.

Pauli's revolutionary proposal was to extend the principle of non-causal events from microphysics (where its legitimacy was recognised) to macrophysics (where it was not). This is why I said that he was more radical in his approach than his colleagues. He probably hoped that, by joining forces with Jung, they would be able to work out some macrophysical theory which made some sense of paranormal events. The attempt was frustrated by deeply ingrained traditions in Western

---

* Cf. Jeans: "The history of physical science in the twentieth century is one of progressive emancipation from the purely human angle of vision."[31]

thought, which go all the way back to the Greeks. Like Kammerer, Jung kept relapsing into spurious causal explanations to make the a-causal principle work. They were both ensnared, as Western man has been for two thousand years, in the logical categories of Greek philosophy which permeate our vocabulary and concepts, and decide for us what is thinkable and what is unthinkable. As Sidney Hook said, "When Aristotle drew up his table of categories, which to him represented the grammar of existence, he was really projecting the grammar of the Greek language on the cosmos."[32] It is that grammar which became the undoing of Kammerer and Jung—together with a host of others who had embarked on a similar quest. The literature of parapsychology is full of hopeful theories which in fact, and for the same reason, were doomed to failure from the beginning.

In Jung's case there is a particular irony because he spent the best part of his life in attempting to translate another untranslatable language into the Western universe of discourse—that of Eastern mysticism. Looking back at the rise and decline of Jungian psychology, it does not seem to have fared better than his theory of non-synchronous synchronicity—but that is a subject beyond the scope of this book.

The upshot of the treatise was a diagram on which, Jung says, he and Pauli "finally agreed". It looks like this:[33]

Indestructible Energy

Constant Connection through Effect (Causality) ← → *Inconstant Connection through Contingence, Similarity, or "Meaning" (Synchronicity)*

Space-Time Continuum

Jung offers no concrete explanations how the schema is meant to work, and his comments on it are so obscure that I must leave it to the interested reader to look them up in the library.[34] One cannot help being reminded of the biblical mountain whose labours gave birth to a mouse: but it was quite a symbolic mouse nevertheless. It was for the first time in the history of modern thought that the hypothesis of a-causal factors working in the universe was given the joint stamp of respectability by a psychologist and a physicist of international renown.

5

There has been in recent years a large crop of other explanatory hypotheses regarding paranormal phenomena. Physicists have played with parallel universes, with Einstein's curved space, with two-dimensional time and "tunnels" in hyper-space which would permit direct contact between regions separated in normal space by astronomical distances. Among psychologists, Freud, once he became convinced of telepathic contact between analyst and patient, theorised that ESP was an archaic method of communication between individuals, which was later supplanted by the more efficient method of sensory communication.* Among biologists a remarkable theory was proposed by Sir Alister Hardy, who thought that the highly skilled and co-ordinated activities

---

* Freud was a member of both the British and the American SPR, and in 1924 wrote to Ernest Jones that he was prepared "to lend the support of psychoanalysis to the matter of telepathy". But Jones feared that this would discredit psychoanalysis and dissuaded Freud from any public gesture. He also prevented Freud from reading, at the International Psychoanalytic Congress in 1922, an essay he had prepared on "Psychoanalysis and Telepathy". It was only published after Freud's death.

of some lower animals, such as the Foraminifera, could only be explained by a kind of group-mind where each individual shared "a psychic blueprint". Among philosophers, Professors Broad and Price have produced challenging mentalistic hypotheses.* Lastly, among mathematicians, G. Spencer Brown proposed an intriguing theory which attempted to explain the anti-chance results in card-guessing experiments by questioning the validity of the concept of chance itself.

Spencer Brown claimed that by matching pairs of digits at random, where the first digit symbolised the guess, and the second the target card, he obtained a significantly higher number of "hits" than chance expectation. However, he did not publish his actual tables, and did not claim that his results were of a comparable magnitude to the astronomical anti-chance odds obtained by the ESP experimenters. The controversy petered out inconclusively, but it nevertheless provided food for thought.† Unlike the propounders of the conspiracy of fraud theory, Spencer Brown admitted that the ESP experiments were "well designed and rigorously controlled"; he accepted the results at face value, but thought that they pointed to some anomaly in the very concept of randomness. Though he did not elaborate on the nature of this suspected anomaly, which was to explain the disproportionately high number of hits in ESP experiments, his ideas bear a close resemblance to Kammerer's concept of Seriality. The "Law of the Series" is in fact the reciprocal of the concept of randomness.

---

* For a summary of these and other explanatory theories see for instance, Rosalind Heywood's *The Sixth Sense* (London, 1959), Appendix.

† Spencer Brown first published his theory in *Nature* (July 25, 1953), "Statistical Significance in Psychical Research", and followed it up in a book, *Probability and Scientific Inference* (London, 1957). See also Rosalind Heywood's brief comment in *The Sixth Sense*, p. 169 f.

It is interesting to note that it was Sir Alister Hardy, a pioneer of ESP research, who provided the grant for Spencer Brown's research. Hardy commented:

> . . . It remained for Mr. G. Spencer Brown of Trinity College, Cambridge, to suggest the alternative and simpler hypothesis that all this experimental work in so-called telepathy, clairvoyance, precognition and psycho-kinesis, which depends upon obtaining results above chance, may be really a demonstration of some single and very different principle. He believes that it may be something no less fundamental or interesting—but not telepathy or these other curious things—something implicit in the very nature and meaning of randomness itself. . . . Whether or not the majority of card-guessing experiments may be shown to be due to something quite different from telepathy, there is to my mind quite sufficient evidence to prove the existence of a true form of telepathy which seems likely to be of considerable biological significance. In passing, let me say that if most of this apparent card-guessing and dice-influencing work should in fact turn out to be something very different, it will not I believe have been a wasted effort; it will have provided a wonderful mine of material for the study of a very remarkable new principle.[35]

That new principle, let me repeat it, looks remarkably like Kammerer's Law of the Series, postulated in 1919. None of the explanatory theories mentioned earlier embraces the whole field of paranormal phenomena. Some accept telepathy, but draw the line at clairvoyance, precognition or PK; and even those "ultras" who accept apparitions and some form of life after death are reluctant to attack the roots of coincidence—although we stumble upon them all the time. I have singled out for discussion Kammerer's Seriality and Jung–Pauli's Synchronicity because they are, to the best of my knowledge, the only theories of the paranormal which do attack the problem of meaningful coincidences.

4
Janus

I

Both Kammerer and Jung postulate an a-causal principle which they consider of equal importance with causality in the destiny of man and of the world at large. The paradoxes of quantum physics may suggest that this postulate is no more preposterous than the theorems of modern science; but even if we were prepared to accept it, we would at once be compelled to ask: what is that a-causal agency up to? What causality is "up to" we think we know quite well: to lend order and stability to the universe which otherwise would be chaotic and unpredictable; to guarantee, as it were, that if I turn on the tap, water will come out and not a sheet of flame. Causality means law and order. But what does the scarab at Jung's window mean?

From antiquity until about the eighteenth century, men had a ready answer to that question in terms of "influences", "sympathies" and "correspondences". The constellations of the planets governed man's character and destiny; macro-cosmos was reflected in micro-cosmos; everything was hanging together, not by mechanical causes but by hidden affinities; there was no room for coincidences in that invisible order. The doctrine of the "sympathy of all things" can be traced all the way back to Hippocrates: "There is one common flow, one common breathing, all things are in sympathy."

It runs like a *leitmotif* through the teaching of the Pythagoreans, the Neo-Platonists and the philosophers of the Renaissance. The dualism of causality and a-causal "sympathy" was neatly summed up by Pico della Mirandola:

Firstly there is the unity in things whereby each thing is at one with itself, consists of itself, and coheres with itself. Secondly, there is the unity whereby one creature is united with the others and all parts of the world constitute one world.[1]*

The Pythagorean concept of the Harmony of the Spheres, revived by the Elizabethans, and the philosophy underlying the pursuits of astrology and alchemy, can all be regarded as variations on the same theme: meaningful coincidences are manifestations of an all-embracing universal order. In Kepler's writings this conception is reflected in its purest form: "Nothing exists nor happens in the visible sky that is not sensed in some hidden manner by the faculties of Earth and Nature: [so that] these faculties of the spirit here on earth are as much affected as the sky itself. . . ."[2] The natural soul of man is not larger in size than a single point, and on this point the form and character of the entire sky is potentially engraved, as if it were a hundred times larger."[3] This capacity of the human soul to act as a cosmic resonator had for Kepler, as it had for Pico, a mystical and a causal aspect: it affirmed the soul's connection with the *anima mundi*, but was at the same time governed by strict geometrical laws.

A century later Leibnitz developed his immensely influential philosophical system centred on the concept of the "monad". The monads, he thought, were "the very

* Pico's third unity is, unavoidably, that of the universe and its Creator.

atoms of nature"; but unlike the material atoms of Democritus, they were spiritual entities, every one a micro-cosmos mirroring the universe in miniature. The monads do not act directly upon one another, "they have no windows by which anything may go in or out", but each is in "accord" or "correspondence" with every other by virtue of a "pre-established harmony".

It was only in the eighteenth century that, in the wake of the Newtonian revolution, causality was enthroned as the absolute ruler of matter and mind—only to be dethroned in the first decades of the twentieth, as a consequence of the revolution in physics. But even in the middle of the materialistic nineteenth century, that lone giant, Arthur Schopenhauer—who had a decisive influence on both Freud and Jung—proclaimed that physical causality was *only one* of the rulers of the world; the other was a metaphysical entity, a kind of universal consciousness, compared to which individual consciousness is as a dream compared to wakefulness:

Coincidence [Schopenhauer wrote] is the simultaneous occurrence of causally unconnected events.... If we visualise each causal chain progressing in time as a meridian on the globe, then we may represent simultaneous events by the parallel circles of latitude. ...[4] All the events in a man's life would accordingly stand in two fundamentally different kinds of connection: firstly, in the objective, causal connection of the natural process; secondly, in a subjective connection which exists only in relation to the individual who experiences it, and which is thus as subjective as his own dreams, whose unfolding content is necessarily determined, but in the manner in which the scenes in a play are determined by the poet's plot. That both kinds of connection exist simultaneously, and the self-same event, although a link in two totally different chains, nevertheless falls into place in both, so that the fate of one individual invariably fits the fate of the other, and each is the hero of his own drama while simultaneously figuring in a drama foreign to him—this is something that surpasses our powers of comprehension, and can only be conceived as possible by virtue of the most wonderful pre-established harmony. . . .[5] It is a great dream dreamt by that single entity, the Will to Life: but in such a way that all his personae must participate in it. Thus everything is interrelated and mutually attuned.[6]

The classical theories of ESP proposed by Carington, Tyrrell, Hardy and others were variations on the same theme—a "psychic ether" or group-mind or collective unconscious, serving as a subterranean pool which individual minds can tap, and through which they can communicate. The dominant concept is Unity in Diversity—all is One and One is all. It echoes through the writings of Christian mystics, and is the keynote in Buddhism and Taosim. It provides the parallels of latitude on Schopenhauer's globe, and ties coincidence into the universal scheme of things. According to Jung, all divinatory practices, from looking at tea-leaves to the complicated oracular methods of the I Ching, are based on the idea that random events are minor mysteries which can be used as pointers towards the one central mystery.

2

Thus Synchronicity and Seriality are modern derivatives of the archetypal belief in the fundamental unity of all things, transcending mechanical causality. Here again modern science provides a curious parallel to the mystical concept of Oneness. One might compare the evolution of science over the last hundred and fifty years to a vast river system, where one tributary after another is swallowed up by the main-stream, and all become unified in a single, majestic river-delta:

> The nineteenth century was the age of the most spectacular syntheses in the history of thought. The science of electricity merged with that of magnetism. Then electro-magnetic radiations were discovered to account for light, colour, radiant heat, Hertzian waves. Chemistry was swallowed up by atomic physics. The control of the body by nerves and glands was seen to rely on electro-chemical processes. The previously independent "effluvia" or "powers of nature" which had been known as "heat", "light", "electric fire" ,"mechanical motion", "magnetic flux", were recognised to be convertible one into another, and to be merely different forms of "energy", whose total amount contained in the universe always remained the same. Soon afterwards, the various forms of matter, the ninety-odd "elements" of chemistry, suffered the same fate, as all atoms were found to be constructed out of the same building blocks in different combinations. And lastly, these building blocks themselves seemed to be nothing but parcels of compressed energy, packed and patterned according to certain mathematical formulae.[7]

The ultimate constituents of the universe: energy and mass, particle and wave, stood thus revealed as different aspects of the same basic process, the same "fundamental Oneness". Whitehead has summed up the situation in a poignant way:

Matter has been identified with energy, and energy is sheer activity. The modern point of view is expressed in terms of energy, activity and the vibratory differentiations of space-time. Any local agitation shakes the whole universe. The distant effects are minute, but they are there. The concept of matter presupposed simple location . . . but in the modern concept the group of agitations which we term matter is fused into its environment. There is no possibility of a detached, self-contained existence.[8]

I have described the parallels between quantum physics and parapsychology as a *negative* affinity—in so far as both are unthinkable, and the weird concepts of one provide an excuse for the weirdness of the other. But the progress of science towards fundamental unity, viewed in a large perspective, provides also a *positive* analogy to the concept of Oneness of the Pythagoreans and their descendants, down to Kammerer and Jung. And perhaps it enables one to gain a better understanding —and a certain forgiveness—for Kammerer's obsession with the idea of a "quasi-gravitational attraction between like and like", "symbiosis", "periodicity", "affinity", and so forth. They are tentative expressions of the inarticulate idea of the "sympathy of all things", of their tendency towards fundamental unity, which the evolution of science reflects on a different level, in its own articulate language. If Kammerer rejected telepathy, it was because he believed that it meant making an unnecessary minor mystery out of phenomena which were included in the major mystery of Seriality—the universal hanging-together of things, their embeddedness in a universal matrix.

3

In the section that follows I shall briefly recapitulate some theoretical considerations set out in previous books,* and try to apply them to the subject of this essay.

I have compared the great syntheses achieved by science over the last hundred and fifty years to a river delta. But each confluence—such as the merging of electricity and magnetism, or of particles and waves—was also followed by a fanning out of more and more specialised branches, subdividing into a network of irrigation channels. To change the metaphor: increasing specialisation is like the branching out of arteries into capillaries; the sequence of mergers is like the reverse confluence of veins. "The cycle which results makes the evolution of ideas appear as a succession of repeated differentiations, specialisations and re-integrations on a higher level—a progression from primordial unity through variety to more complex patterns of unity-in-variety."[9]

This dual aspect in the evolution of science reflects a basic polarity in nature itself: differentiation and integration. In the growing embryo, successive generations of cells branch out into diversified tissues, which eventually become integrated into organs. Every organ has the dual character of being a subordinate part and at the same time an autonomous whole—which will continue to function even if transplanted into another host. The individual itself is an organic whole, but at the same time a part of his family or tribe. Each social group has again the characteristics of a coherent whole but also of a dependent part within the community or nation. Parts

* The Ghost in the Machine (London, 1967) and Beyond Reductionism—New Perspectives in the Life Sciences. The Alpbach Symposium, ed. A. Koestler and J. R. Smythies (London, 1969).

and wholes in an absolute sense do not exist anywhere. The living organism and the body social are not assemblies of elementary bits; they are multi-levelled, hierarchically organised systems of sub-wholes containing sub-wholes of a lower order, like Chinese boxes.* These sub-wholes—or "holons", as I have proposed to call them†—are Janus-faced entities which display both the independent properties of wholes and the dependent properties of parts. Each holon must preserve and assert its autonomy, otherwise the organism would lose its articulation and dissolve into an amorphous mass— but at the same time the holon must remain subordinate to the demands of the (existing or evolving) whole. "Autonomy" in this context means that organelles, cells, muscles, nerves, organs, all have their intrinsic rhythm and pattern of functioning, aided by self-regulatory devices; and that they tend to persist in and assert their characteristic patterns of activity. This *self-assertive tendency* is a fundamental and universal characteristic of holons, manifested on every level, from cells to individuals to social groups.

On the other hand, the activities of holons are initiated, inhibited or modified by controls on higher levels of the hierarchy. The pace-maker system of the heart, for instance, is controlled by the autonomic nervous system and by hormones; these in turn depend on orders from centres in the brain which may overrule and interfere with the routine functions of the subordinate centres. Thus the *self-assertive tendency* of the holon has its counterpart in its *integrative tendency* to function as part of the larger whole.

The polarity of these two tendencies, or potentials, is

---

* The term "hierarchy" refers to the type of organisation usually diagrammed as a pyramid or an inverted tree, e.g. on administration charts; or alternatively as a multiple system of Chinese boxes.
† From the Greek *holos*—whole—with the suffix *on* suggesting a part.

a ubiquitous phenomenon in all domains of life. In the multiplicity of social hierarchies, the self-assertive tendencies are manifested on different levels as selfishness, clannishness, nationalism, and so on; the integrative tendencies as altruism, co-operativeness, internationalism —in general, subordination to the interests of the next higher level in the hierarchy. The stability of organisms and societies depends on the proper balance between the opposite tendencies of its holons. Under normal conditions, the two are in dynamic equilibrium. Under conditions of stress, the affected part of an organism may tend to escape the restraining controls of the whole. The same applies to social groups which, when tension exceeds a critical limit, tend to assert themselves to the detriment of the whole. Vice versa, the whole may exercise an over-strict control of the parts, making them lose their individuality.

This basic polarity is not a metaphysical postulate, but a direct consequence of the dual nature of every stable biological unit as a self-reliant whole and as a dependent part of a larger whole. The self-asserting tendencies of the Janus-faced holon are derived from the former, its integrative tendencies from the latter. Janus also reigns in inanimate nature. In quantum physics, the Principle of Complementarity ascribes to sub-atomic entities a dual nature—the capacity to behave as a particle, a small, compact whole, and alternatively as a wave-function of the Nirvana-like psi field. In the universe at large, stability is maintained by the equilibration of opposite forces: inertial, centrifugal tendencies represent the independent properties of parts within the cosmic hierarchy, from galaxies down to molecules; while the cohesive forces, electro-magnetic or gravitational, keep the part in its place in the larger whole.

On the ladder of organic evolution, the manifestations of the integrative tendency range from symbiosis and colonialism to the cohesive forces in flocks and herds, to the integrative bonds in insect-states, and lastly to the sexual ties and social hierarchies of primates and men. The self-assertive tendencies form a similar range: plants compete for light and space, animal species compete for ecological niches, and within each species there is competition for territory, dominance, mates and food.

The forces through which the basic polarity manifests itself vary on each level, but there is nevertheless the same pattern running through the whole gamut. The two faces of Janus: one, that of a proud, self-asserting whole, the other of a humble integrated part, yield a serviceable pair of symbols. It certainly has a wider range of applicability than Freud's pair of Ultimates—Eros and Thanatos. The sex-drive appears in our view as only one among many other integrative forces in both animal and human societies; while aggression and destructiveness appear, not as primary instincts, but pathological flare-ups of the self-assertive tendencies under conditions of abnormal stress. Both Eros and Thanatos appear only relatively late on the stage of evolution: creatures that multiply by fission or budding are ignorant of sex and death. The great duet in Freud's metapsychology does not constitute the whole opera.*

4

The starting point of this excursion into system-theory was the quest for ultimate Unity, shared by the physicist, the mystic and the parapsychologist; a kind of unity which can only be attained by a detour through diversity, on a higher turn of the spiral. Among biologists, too, there is

* For a discussion of Freud's metapsychology see *Insight and Outlook*, Chapters X, XV and XVI.

a revival of interest in the potentials of living matter to build up forms of greater complexity which display unity-in-variety on a higher level—in other words, in the integrative powers of life, as distinct from the conception of evolution-through-chance-mutations.

These powers are perhaps most strikingly demonstrated at the very bottom of the evolutionary ladder. A classic example is the behaviour of the slime mould, of which John Bleibtreu has recently given a graphic description.* The slime mould is an amoeba which lives on bacteria found among the decaying leaves in forests. It multiplies by simple cell division every few hours. This leads to recurrent population explosions accompanied by shortage of food. When threatened by famine, the amoeba "commence the enactment of an incredible series of activities. These activities are a literal metaphor for the organisation of cells in a multi-celled individual, or the organisation of individuals into a social unit."

The amoeba stop behaving as individuals and aggregate into groups, which form clumps, discernible to the naked eye. These clumps then "form straggling streamers of living matter, which . . . orient themselves towards central collection points. . . . At the hub of each central aggregation point, a mound begins to form as groups of amoeba mount themselves atop other groups. . . . This hub gradually rises first into the shape of a blunt peg, and then into a distinctly phallic erection. When all the incoming streams of amoeba are almost completely incorporated into this erected cartridge-like form, it topples over onto its side, now looking like a slimy sausage. This slug begins now to migrate across the forest floor to a point where, hopefully, more favourable ecological conditions will prevail. Estimations about the size of the population . . . vary, but generally it is thought that perhaps some half a million amoeba are involved.

* *The Parable of the Beast* (New York, 1968).

. . . After migrating for a variable period of time (which can be two minutes or two weeks) in the direction of light and warmth, this slug gradually erects itself once again into its phallic shape until it is standing on its tail. . . . This oval shape gradually assumes the form of a candle flame, bellied at the bottom and coming to a point at the top. . . . The end result is a delicate tapering shaft capped by a spherical mass of spores. When the spores are dispersed . . . each can split open to liberate a tiny new amoeba."[10]

Are the amoeba, so long as they hunt alone, whole individuals—which then become transformed into parts of the slug? Are the polyps which specialise as tentacles, floats or genitals of the Portuguese Man of War, individuals or organs? Are bees and termites, whose existence is completely controlled by the interests of the group, possessed of a group mind?

Sponges and hydras—fresh-water polyps—are primitive forms of animal life. If a living sponge, or hydra, is crushed to pulp, passed through a fine filter, then poured into water, the pulp soon aggregates into flat sheets, then curls into balls which end up as adult individuals, equipped with normal mouth, tentacles and so forth.

The integrative powers of living matter seem like magic. A flatworm can be cut into virtually as many segments as you like, and each segment will regenerate a complete individual. Similar regenerative powers are found in the embryonic tissues of higher animals. If in a frog embryo the eye-cup, destined to grow into the future eye, is cut into fragments, each fragment will form a smaller, complete eye. If the eye-cup is transplanted to the belly of the frog-embryo, the skin over it will obligingly differentiate into a lens. If tissue from a chick embryo in its early stages is submitted to the same mincing and filtering treatment as the sponge and transplanted to the membrane of another chick embryo, the scrambled liver cells will start forming a liver, the kidney cells a kidney, the skin cells feathers.

These and other laboratory experiments show in miniature, as it were, the manifestations of the Integrative Tendency in embryonic development, regeneration and social co-operation—from the slime mould to the bee. In each case there are causal factors at work—but they obey laws specific to living substance, which are not found in the realms of inanimate matter. The gospel of classical physics was the so-called Second Law of Thermo-Dynamics—according to which the universe is running down like a clock because all its energy is being steadily dissipated into the random motion of molecules in a gas—so that the end would be as the beginning was according to *Genesis*: "without form and void". Only in recent years did biologists realise that this law applies only in the theoretical case of a "closed system", completely isolated from its environment; whereas all living organisms are "open systems" which feed on energies and materials found in their environment. Instead of *running down* like a clockwork which dissipates energy through friction, a living organism is all the time *building up* more complex chemicals from the chemicals it feeds on, more complex forms of energy from the energy it absorbs, and more complex patterns of "information"—perceptions, memories, ideas—from the input of its receptors. It is active instead of being just reactive; it adapts the environment to its needs, instead of passively adapting to it; it learns from experience and constructs systems of knowledge out of the chaos of sensations impinging on it; it sucks information from the environment as it feeds on its substances and synthesises its energies.

The same integrative "building-up" tendency is manifested in the evolution of species towards more complex forms of physique and behaviour, more efficient ways of communication, with greater independence from and mastery of the environment. To quote von Bertalanffy, one of the pioneers of the new outlook in the biological sciences: "According to the Second Law of Thermo-Dynamics, the general direction of physical events is towards decrease of order and organisation. In contrast to this, a direction towards increasing order seems to be present in evolution."[11]

This tendency towards "increasing order"—a higher form of unity in a more complex variety—I have called the "Integrative Tendency". In the present theory it is regarded as an "ultimate and irreducible" principle in nature, complementary to the equally basic Self-Asserting Tendency of its individual holons. I hope to have shown, at the risk of boring the reader, that the concept is firmly anchored in the biological sciences, and more than an *ad hoc* hypothesis.

5

The human individual, too, is a Janus-faced holon. Looking inward, he sees himself as a self-contained, unique whole; looking outward, as a dependent part of his natural and social environment. His self-assertive tendencies are the dynamic manifestations of his experience of wholeness; his integrative tendency is a manifestation of his partness.

The polarity is reflected in his emotive behaviour. Self-assertion finds its outlets in ambition, competitiveness, aggressive-defensive behaviour, according to the stresses to which the individual is exposed. His integrative potential, on the other hand, may find its fulfilment through identification with family, community or some other social group. But it can also express itself in a craving to surrender to something that is larger than society and transcends the boundaries of the self—which may be God, or nature, or a Bach cantata, or the mystic's "oceanic feeling". We may call this category of emotions, derived from the integrative tendency, the *self-transcending emotions*. They are experienced as devotion, empathy, identification, hypnotic rapport. Going one step further, we may include into this category the trance-states of mystics and mediums, the effects of certain psychotropic drugs, and the emotions which accompany spontaneous paranormal experiences.

But these are rare events. Under ordinary circumstances, both self-asserting and self-transcending impulses enter in various proportions into our emotive experiences. "Love"—sexual or maternal—usually contains an aggressive or possessive, and an identificatory, component. In the scientist, ambition is balanced with devotion to the task. Even the act of feeding has a self-transcending component—the mystic belief of Primitives in sharing the virtues of the devoured enemy, animal or god, and in the rituals of conviviality.

As I have discussed this subject at length in several previous books, I shall not cover the same ground again, but rather quote an extract from *The Ghost in the Machine*:

The self-transcending emotions show a wide range of variety. They may be joyous or sad, tragic or lyrical; their common denominator, to repeat this once more, is the feeling of *integrative participation in an experience which transcends the boundaries of the self*.

Self-assertive emotions tend towards bodily activity; the self-transcending emotions are essentially passive and cathartic. To be "overwhelmed" by awe and wonder, "enraptured" by a smile, "entranced" by beauty—each of these words expresses passive surrender, and a craving to transcend the island boundaries of the individual, to enter into symbiotic communion with a human being, living or dead, or some higher entity, real or imaginary, of which the self is felt to be a part.

Freud and Piaget, among others, have emphasised that the very young child does not differentiate between ego and environment. It is aware of events, but not of itself as a separate entity. It lives in a state of mental symbiosis with the outer world, a continuation of the biological symbiosis in the womb. The universe is focussed on the self, and the self *is* the universe—a condition which Piaget called "protoplasmic" or "symbiotic" consciousness, and which may be at the origin of that "oceanic feeling" which the artist and the mystic strive to recapture on a higher level of development, at a higher turn of the spiral. Symbiotic consciousness is never completely defeated, merely relegated underground to those primitive strata in the mental hierarchy where the boundaries of the ego are still fluid and blurred. It survives in the sympathetic magic of primitives, the belief in transubstantiation, the mystic bonds which unite a person with his tribe, his totem, his shadow, his effigy, and later with his god. In the major Eastern philosophies, the "I am thou and thou art me", the identity of the "Real Self" with the Atman, the all-one, has been preserved throughout the ages.[12]

5
The Country of the Blind

I

And thus, after several detours, we are back at our starting point. The mystic's "oceanic feeling" is certainly on a higher turn of the spiral than the new-born infant's; the infant has not yet attained personal identity, the mystic and the medium have transcended it. There are many turns to the spiral, from the slime-mould upward; but at each turn we are confronted with the same polarity, the same Janus-faced holons, one face of which says I am the centre of the world, the other, I am a part in search of the whole.

We may regard the phenomena of parapsychology as the rewards of this search—whether produced spontaneously or in the laboratory. ESP would then appear as the highest manifestation of the integrative potential of living matter—which, on the human level, is typically accompanied by a self-transcending type of emotion. Whereas throughout our excursion into biology and physics we were on solid scientific ground, this is a speculative step, and I do not pretend it to be more. But it is modern science itself, with its paradoxical vistas, which encourages one to take it.

Nor should we stop at "classical" ESP—telepathy and short-term precognition—for which some physicalistic explanations may still be found. To exclude clairvoyance, PK and serial or synchronistic coincidences would be arbitrary, and leave things as they stood before. On the other hand, by regarding the Integrative Tendency as a universal principle which includes a-causal phenomena, the picture becomes greatly simplified, even if still beyond the grasp of understanding. Instead of several mysteries, we are now faced with a single, irreducible evolutionary tendency towards building up more complex wholes out of more diversified parts. The Hippocratic doctrine of the "sympathy of all things" was an early paradigm for it; the evolution of knowledge, with its fannings out into specialised branches, and their confluence into the unified delta, is another. One might indeed substitute for the awkward terms "Seriality" and "Synchronicity" —with their misplaced emphasis on time alone—the non-committal expression "confluential events". Confluential events would be a-causal manifestations of the Integrative Tendency. The appearance of Jung's scarab would be a confluential event. So would be the psychokinetic effects on rolling dice, and other paranormal, a-causal phenomena. What lends them significance is that they *give the impression* of being causally connected, though they demonstrably are not—a kind of pseudo-causality. The scarab seems to be *attracted* to Jung's window by the patient telling her dream; the dice seem to be *manipulated* by the experimenter's will; the clairvoyant seems to *see* the cards hidden from him. The Integrative potentials of life seem to include the capacity of producing pseudo-causal effects—of bringing about a confluential event without bothering, so to speak, to employ physical agencies.

It is, however, not always easy to draw a sharp line separating causal from non-causal events. Sightless animals must feel their way by the coarse physical agencies of touch, perhaps aided by smell. Bats employ a kind of radar—which not so long ago would have struck naturalists as a very wild hypothesis. Animals equipped with eyes react to photons—to particles with zero rest-mass which can also behave like waves in a non-medium and thus seem to defy causality. A species of humans without eyes—such as the citizens of Wells' *Country of the Blind*—would surely reject our claim of being able to perceive distant objects, without contact by touch, as occult nonsense—or else declare that such a faculty, if it really exists, is definitely beyond the realm of physical causality, and should be called extra-sensory perception.

2

One of Britain's most respected neurophysiologists, Dr. W. Grey Walter, performed in recent years a remarkable series of experiments. In his 1969 Eddington Memorial Lecture he reported, laconically, that "harnessed to an electric machine, by an effort of will, one can influence external events without movement or overt action through the impalpable electric surges of one's own brain". This effort "requires a peculiar state of concentration, a paradoxical compound of detachment and excitement".[1]

Grey Walter's experimental procedure can be described, in a simplified way, as follows. The electrodes attached to the scalp over the subject's frontal cortex transmit his electrical brain-activities through an amplifier to the machine. In front of the subject there is a button: if he presses it down an "interesting scene" will appear on a TV screen. Approximately one second before he presses the button, an electric surge of about twenty micro-volts occurs in a large area of the subject's cortex; this is known as the "readiness wave". But the circuits of the apparatus can be so adjusted that the amplified "readiness wave" is in itself sufficient to trigger a switch and make the TV scene appear a fraction of a second *before* the subject has actually pressed the button. This is called "auto-start":

> An intelligent subject soon realises that his intended action has had the expected result *before* he has actually moved his finger, and usually ceases to bother to press the button: the pictures appear as and when he wants them. . . . For this effect to be sustained it is essential that the subject should really "want" the event to occur, and concentrate on evoking this particular event. When the subject's attention wanders with monotonous presentation, or he "concentrates on concentration", the brain potential fails to rise and he receives no pictures. Auto-start can be combined with auto-stop so that the subject can acquire a picture by willing its appearance on the TV screen, and then erase it as soon as he has completed his inspection of it.
>
> From the standpoint of the subject this is a very peculiar experience, sometimes accompanied by signs of suppressed excitement; diuresis [discharge of urine] has been very marked in two of the experimenters while acting as subjects for these trials.[2]

Reviewing Grey Walter's experiments, Renée Haynes, editor of the journal of the SPR, commented:

> In principle, of course, this is no more remarkable than what happens when a child wonderingly looks at its hand and decides to prove the power of its will by resolving to move a finger and moving it. In practice it is astonishing because this [Grey Walter's] mode of exerting influence over the outer world is so unfamiliar in man, however commonplace it may be to the electric eel. It is also fascinating in that it has

led Dr. Grey Walter, with some embarrassment, to use "such a word as willpower".[3]

This, we remember, was also the attitude of Sir John Eccles when he regarded the action of "mental will" on "physical brain" as the basic mystery, and PK merely as an extension of it. One might describe Grey Walter's experiment as "pseudo-telekinesis" because there are wires connecting the electrodes on the subject's skull with the TV apparatus. But one might equally well describe the action of the subject's mind on his own brain as pseudo-causality. Or we might say that the subject has discovered a more elegant way of producing a "confluential event", without bothering to employ physical agencies.

3

A word should be said in this context about the hypnotic rapport. Until the middle of the last century, hypnosis was treated as an occult fancy by Western science (although in other cultures it was taken for granted); today it has become so respectable and commonplace that we are apt to forget that we have no explanation for it. The evidence shows that a suitable subject can be made temporarily deaf, dumb, blind, anaesthetised, induced to experience hallucinations, or re-live scenes from his past. He can be made to forget or remember what happened during the trance at a snap of fingers. He can be given a post-hypnotic suggestion which will make him perform the following day, at 5 p.m. precisely, some silly action like untying his shoelaces—and then find some rationalisation for it.

The uses of medical hypnosis on suitable patients in

dentistry, obstetrics and dermatology are well known.* Less well known, however, are the experiments by A. Mason and S. Black on the suppression of allergic skin responses by hypnosis. Patients were injected with extracts of pollen, to which they were known to be allergic, and after hypnotic treatment, ceased to show any reaction. In other patients hypnosis suppressed the allergic reaction against the tubercle bacillus. How hypnotic suggestions can alter the chemical reactivity of tissues on the microscopic level is anybody's guess. After Mason's remarkable cure by hypnosis of a boy of sixteen suffering from ichthyosis (fish-skin disease, a congenital affliction previously thought to be incurable) a reviewer in the *British Medical Journal* commented that this single case was enough to require "a revision of current concepts on the relation between mind and body".

4

That revision of current concepts is long overdue. We do not know whether Eddington was right when he said that the world is made of mind-stuff, but is it certainly not made of the stuff of the nineteenth-century physicist's little billiard balls flying around at random until chance makes them aggregate into an amoeba. In his 1969 Address to the American Society for Psychical Research, which I have quoted before, Professor Henry Margenau had this to say:

* Although its clinical applications are limited by the fact that complete anaesthesis can only be induced in "deep" trance, and that apparently only five per cent of the population are "deep" trance subjects, while about thirty-five per cent can be put into a medium trance, and nearly everybody into a light trance.[4]

An artifact occasionally invoked to explain precognition is to make time multidimensional. This allows a genuine backward passage of time, which might permit positive intervals in one time direction to become negative ("effect before cause") in another. In principle, this represents a valid scheme, and I know of no criticism that will rule it out as a scientific procedure. If it is to be acceptable, however, a completely new metric of space-time needs to be developed. . . .

I have probed physics for suggestions it can offer towards a solution of the sort of problem you seem to encounter. The positive results, I fear, are meagre and disappointing, though perhaps worth inspection. But why, I should now like to ask, is it necessary to import into any new discipline all the approved concepts of an older science in its contemporary stage of development? Physics did not adhere slavishly to the Greek rationalistic formulations that preceded it; it was forced to create its own specific constructs. . . .

The parapsychologist, I think . . . must strike out on his own and probably reason in bolder terms than present-day physics suggest—tolerate the strident critical voices of hard-boiled, pragmatic, and satisfied scientists without too much concern, and continue his own painstaking search for an understanding of new kinds of experience, possibly in terms of concepts which now appear strange[5] [compressed].

We are surrounded by phenomena whose existence we studiously ignore; or, if they cannot be ignored, dismiss as superstitions. Until the thirteenth century man did not realise that he was surrounded by magnetic forces. Nor do we have any direct sensory awareness of them; nor of the showers of neutrinos which traverse us;

nor of other unknown "influences". So we might just
as well listen to Margenau's advice and create "our own
specific constructs" by assuming that we live immersed
in some sort of "psycho-magnetic field" which produces
confluential events by means transcending the classical
concepts of physics. Its purpose and design are unknown
to us, but we feel it to be somehow related to that striving
towards higher forms of order and unity-in-variety
which we observe in the evolution of the universe at
large, of life on earth, human consciousness, and lastly
science and art. One ultimate mystery is easier to accept
than a litter-box of unrelated puzzles. It does not explain
why the scarab appeared at the window, but at least it
fits confluential events and other paranormal phenomena
into a unified design.

There is, however, one profoundly disturbing aspect
to these phenomena. Paranormal events are rare, unpredictable and capricious. That, as we saw, is the main
reason why sceptics feel justified in rejecting the results
of card-guessing and PK experiments, in spite of the
statistical evidence which, in any other field of research,
would be sufficient to prove the hypothesis.

One reason for the erratic nature of ESP has already
been mentioned: our inability to control the unconscious
processes underlying it. Grey Walter's experiments were
not concerned with ESP, yet he had to realise that the
"readiness wave" will only attain sufficient strength if
the subject is in a state described as "a paradoxical
compound of detachment and excitement". Spontaneous
paranormal experiences are always bound up with some
self-transcending type of emotion, as in telepathic
dreams or in mediumistic trance; and in the laboratory,
too, emotional rapport between experimenter and subject
is of decisive importance. The subject's interest in the
mystery of ESP in itself evokes a self-transcending
emotion; when that interest flags at the end of a long

ESP sitting, there is a characteristic falling-off in the number of "hits" on the score-sheet. This "decline effect" (p. 123) is regarded as an additional proof for the reality of ESP. There is also an overall decline in the performance of most subjects after a prolonged series of sittings. They get bored. Most normal skills improve with practice. In ESP the opposite is the case.

5

A further argument relating to the apparent *rarity* of paranormal phenomena was put forward by the late Professor Broad in an article in *Philosophy*:

> If paranormal cognition and paranormal causation are facts, then it is quite likely that they are not confined to those very rare occasions on which they either manifest themselves sporadically in a spectacular way, or to those very special conditions in which their presence can be experimentally established. They may well be continually operating in the background of our normal lives. Our understanding of, and our misunderstandings with, our fellow men; our general emotional mood on certain occasions; the ideas which suddenly arise in our minds without any obvious introspectable cause; our unaccountable immediate emotional reactions towards certain persons; . . . and so on; all these may be in part determined by paranormal cognition and paranormal causal influences.[6]

Broad's colleague at Oxford, Professor H. H. Price, added an interesting suggestion regarding the apparent *capriciousness* of ESP:

It looks as if telepathically received impressions have some difficulty in crossing the threshold and manifesting themselves in consciousness. There seems to be some barrier or repressive mechanism which tends to shut them out from consciousness, a barrier which is rather difficult to pass, and they make use of all sorts of devices for overcoming it. Sometimes they make use of the muscular mechanisms of the body, and emerge in the form of automatic speech or writing. Sometimes they emerge in the form of dreams, sometimes as visual or auditory hallucinations. And often they can only emerge in a distorted and symbolic form (as other unconscious mental contents do). It is a plausible guess that many of our everyday thoughts and emotions are telepathic or partly telepathic in origin, but are not recognised to be so because they are so much distorted and mixed with other mental contents in crossing the threshold of consciousness.[7]

Adrian Dobbs, commenting on this passage, raised an important point:

This is a very interesting and suggestive passage. It evokes the picture of either the mind or the brain as containing an assemblage of selective filters, designed to cut out unwanted signals on neighbouring frequencies, some of which get through in a distorted form, just as in ordinary radio reception.[8]

6

The "filter theory", as one might call it, actually goes back to Henri Bergson, and has been taken up by various writers on extra-sensory perception. It is in fact simply an extrapolation from what we know about ordinary sensory perception. Our main sense organs are like narrow slits which admit only a very narrow frequency-range of electro-magnetic and sound waves. But even the amount that does get in through these narrow slits is too much. Life would be impossible if we were to pay attention to the millions of stimuli bombarding our senses—what William James called "the blooming, buzzing multitude of sensations". Thus the nervous system, and above all the brain, functions as a hierarchy of filtering and classifying devices which eliminate a large proportion of the sensory input as irrelevant "noise", and process the relevant information into manageable shape before it is presented to consciousness. An oft-quoted example of this filtering process is the "cocktail-party phenomenon" which enables us to isolate a single voice in the general buzz.

By analogy, a similar filtering mechanism might be assumed to protect us from the blooming, buzzing multitude of images, messages, impressions and confluential happenings in the "psycho-magnetic field" surrounding us. Since this is a point of great importance in trying to understand why paranormal phenomena present themselves in such inexplicable and arbitrary guises, I shall indulge in a few more quotations relevant to it. Thus the psychiatrist James S. Hayes, writing in *The Scientist Speculates*:*

* Ed. I. J. Good (London, 1962).

I have long felt that the conventional questions asked about telepathy ("Does it occur, and if so, how?") are less likely to be fruitful than the question: "If telepathy occurs at all, what prevents it from occurring all the time? How does the mind (or the brain) insulate itself from the potential influx of other people's experiences?"[9]

Next, Sir Cyril Burt again:

. . . Man's natural conception of the universe, or rather of the restricted portion of it with which he has to cope, is that of a world of tangible objects of moderate size, moving about with moderate speeds in a visible three-dimensional container under the impact of contact forces (the push and pull of simple mechanical interactions), all in accordance with fairly simple laws. Until quite recently this has also been the conception of the universe adopted by the scientist. His criterion for reality . . . was that of the Doubting Thomas: what can be seen or touched. Yet to suppose that on such a basis we can construct a complete and all-inclusive picture of the universe is like supposing that a street-plan of Rome will tell you what the Eternal City looks like when you get there.

" 'Osses," said the coachman to Tom Brown, " 'as to wear blinkers, so's they see only wot's in front of 'em: and that's the safest plan for 'umble folk like you and me." Nature seems to have worked on much the same principle. Our sense organs and our brain operate as an intricate kind of filter which limits and directs the mind's clairvoyant powers, so that under normal conditions attention is concentrated on just those objects or situations that are of biological importance for the survival of the organism and its species. . . . As a rule, it would seem, the mind rejects ideas coming from another mind as the body rejects grafts coming from another body.[10]

Burt sums up his views by reminding us that contemporary physics recognises four types of interactions ("strong", "weak", electro-magnetic and gravitational), each of which

obeys its own laws, and so far at any rate has defeated all attempts to reduce it to any other type. This being so, there can be no antecedent improbability which forbids us postulating yet another system and yet another type of interaction, awaiting more intensive investigation—a psychic universe consisting of events or entities linked by psychic interactions, obeying laws of their own and interpenetrating the physical universe and partly overlapping, much as the various interactions already discovered and recognised overlap each other.[11]

7

The preceding section may have evoked in the reader a feeling of *déjà vu*, because earlier on (p. 82) I mentioned another type of "filter theory" related to Evolution. I am referring to the neo-Darwinian theory, according to which the hereditary substance in the germ cells is protected by an almost inviolable barrier against influences originating in the outside world. The "almost" refers to cosmic rays, noxious heat, and chemicals which might penetrate the barrier and cause mutations in the genes. Most of these are harmful, but from time to time there are lucky hits, and these, with the aid of natural selection, keep the wheels of evolution turning. Apart from that, any possibility of some acquired characteristic becoming hereditary is prevented by the barrier. Lamarckism, which postulated that beneficial improvements in physique or skills acquired by the parents could be transmitted to the offspring, must be discarded as an unscientific superstition.

This is the neo-Darwinian doctrine. And yet certain evolutionary phenomena, quoted over and again in the literature, seem to point stubbornly at some Lamarckian factor in evolution. A simple example is the skin on the soles of our feet, which is much thicker than elsewhere. If the thickening occurred while the baby learned to walk, there would be no problem. But the thickening is inherited, the baby is born with it. Equally puzzling are the inborn callosities on the camel's knee, and the bulbous thickenings on the ostrich's undercarriage, one fore, one aft, on which the ostrich squats. These too are, like the skin on our soles, already present in the embryo; they are undeniably inherited characteristics. Yet in conformity with the prevailing dogma, we are asked to believe that the advent of these callosities at the exact spots where the animal needed them was due to pure chance—like the scarab appearing at Jung's window.

One could almost substitute ESP for IAC (Inheritance of Acquired Characters) to see the same pattern of argument emerging, and the same quasi-theological passions accompanying it. The Lamarckians found themselves in a predicament similar to the parapsychologists': they were unable to produce a repeatable experiment. Cases of apparent IAC in the animal kingdom were rare, the phenomena were capricious; each apparently clear-cut case was open to different interpretations— and as a last resort, to accusations of fraud. Moreover, though the Lamarckians were convinced that IAC did occur, they were unable to provide a physiological explanation for it—as parapsychologists are unable to provide a physical explanation for ESP.

This curious parallel seems to have escaped the attention of both Lamarckians and parapsychologists; I have not seen it mentioned in the literature. Perhaps one heresy is enough for one man. Paul Kammerer shared both; yet he, too, seems to have been unaware of the connection between them.

Let us carry the analogy one step further. In *The Ghost in the Machine* and *The Case of the Midwife Toad* I have discussed the reasons for a growing discontent with Neo-Darwinian theory among contemporary biologists who believe that the theory reflects part of the picture, but not the whole picture, and who maintain that the evolution of species is the combined result of a whole spectrum of causative factors, some known, most of them unknown. Darwinian inheritance, and a modified form of Lamarckian inheritance, might be two such factors at opposite ends of the spectrum, both with a limited field of applicability. Lamarckian IAC would be a relatively rare event—and for the same reason that ESP phenomena are rare: the operation of protective filters. These would not constitute the absolute barrier stipulated by the orthodox theory, but selective mechanisms, protecting the hereditary material against the "blooming, buzzing confusion" of biochemical incursions, which would otherwise play havoc with the continuity and stability of the species. If every experience of the ancestors left its hereditary trace on the offspring, the result would inevitably be a chaos of shapes and a bedlam of instincts. But this does not mean that we must exclude the possibility that some well-defined, purposeful adaptations—the ostrich's callosities, for instance—which were acquired by generation after generation, should eventually seep through the filter and lead to changes in the chemistry of genes which made them inheritable. It seems very unlikely that philogeny should possess no memory. Biochemistry does not exclude the above possibility;* and the almost fanatical insistence on its rejection is but one more example of the dogmatic intolerance of scientific orthodoxies.

8

We have to make one last excursion into physics—but this time of a very elementary kind.

On the shadow desk in front of me there is a shadow ashtray. For ordinary purposes it is quite a sensible, solid object, a whole in itself, with no quantum nonsense about it. But when I lift it, I feel its weight, which means that it is subject to a rather mysterious influence which we call the earth's gravitational field. And when I push it, it resists. This is partly due to the friction against the desk, but partly to the massive ashtray's inertia. Now inertia is defined, according to Newton's First Law of Motion, as the tendency of a body to preserve its state of rest or uniform motion in a given direction. But if I were to suspend my ashtray on a fine thread from the ceiling, and turn it into a replica of Foucault's pendulum in the Paris Invalides, the plane of its oscillations would not remain fixed in its given direction, as the principle of inertia requires, but would slowly rotate, completing a turn in twenty-four hours. We explain that this is caused by the earth's rotation, and that my ashtray pendulum *did* preserve its direction *relative to the fixed stars,* so all is well. However, since all motion is relative, we are entitled to regard the earth at rest, and the fixed

* An eminent member of the Establishment, Professor Waddington, actually proposed some years ago a tentative model for IAC, indicating that at the present stage of biochemistry such a process is conceivable.[12]

stars revolving around it—as the ancients did; and if this is the case, why should my ashtray's motions be governed by the stars, instead of the earth below it? The same argument applies to the flattening of the earth's poles, and the so-called Coriolus force which deflects missiles, jet planes and trade winds from their straight inertial direction. They all seem to demonstrate that the earth's rotation is absolute, not relative.

This paradox was first pointed out by Bishop Berkeley, then by the German physicist Ernst Mach (after whom the units of supersonic speed are named). Mach's answer was that we are indeed entitled to regard the earth as at rest, and to explain the phenomena which we ascribed to its rotation as somehow caused by the fixed stars and galaxies—that is, by the mass of the universe around us. According to this theory, known as Mach's Principle, it is the universe around us which determines the direction of Foucault's pendulum, and governs the inertial forces on earth responsible for the flattening of the poles. Einstein took over Mach's Principle and postulated that the inertia of earthly bodies is merely another manifestation of gravity, not due to the stars as such, but rather to their rotation. This is the accepted theory today. *How* the rotation of the stars produces the inertia of my ashtray is anybody's guess.

Inertia is the most tangible, down-to-earth phenomenon in our daily existence: you are up against it whenever you shift a piece of furniture. And yet it has now been discovered that its resistance to being shifted is due to the circumstance that it is surrounded by the rotating mass of the universe. In 1927, Bertrand Russell, though subscribing to Einsteinian Relativity, nevertheless felt impelled to protest:

It is urged that for "absolute rotation" we may substitute "rotation relative to the fixed stars". This is formally correct, but the influence attributed to the fixed stars savours of astrology, and is scientifically incredible.[13]

Whitehead wrote in the same vein:

It is difficult to take seriously the suggestion that these domestic phenomena on the earth are due to the influence of the fixed stars. I cannot persuade myself to believe that a little star in its twinkling turned round Foucault's pendulum in the Paris Exhibition of 1851.[14]

Thus even my ashtray is a holon, after all. It is not merely a shadow ashtray on an Eddington shadow desk; but in some way, for which neither Mach nor Einstein ventured to give a causal explanation, its inertial properties are connected with the whole mass of the universe around it. One might as well call it a Mirandola ashtray, remembering the passage quoted earlier on:

Firstly there is the unity in things whereby each thing is at one with itself, consists of itself, and coheres with itself. Secondly, there is the unity whereby one creature is united with the .others, and all parts of the world constitute one world.[15]

9

We have heard a whole chorus of Nobel Laureates in physics informing us that matter is dead, causality is dead, determinism is dead. If that is so, let us give them a decent burial, with a requiem of electronic music. It is time for us to draw the lessons from twentieth-century post-mechanistic science, and to get out of the strait-jacket which nineteenth-century materialism imposed on our philosophical outlook. Paradoxically, had that outlook kept abreast with modern science itself, instead of lagging a century behind it, we would have been liberated from that strait-jacket long ago.

It has been said that science knows more and more about less and less. But that applies only to the fanning-out process of specialisation. One would be equally justified in saying that we know less and less about more and more. That applies to the complementary process of the unification of matter and energy, particle and waves into one conceptual river delta, majestically moving into an ocean of abstractions—for the more precise knowledge science acquired, the more elusive became the symbols it had to use. The hunting of the quark begins to resemble the mystic's quest for the cloud of unknowing. Science turns out to be the most glorious achievement of the human mind—and its most tantalising defeat. We have become a good deal cleverer since Pico della Mirandola, but not much wiser in knowing what it all means.

But once this is recognised, we might become more receptive to phenomena around us which a one-sided emphasis on physical science has made us ignore; might feel the draught that is blowing through the chinks of the causal edifice; pay more attention to confluential events; include the paranormal phenomena in our concept of normality; and realise that we have been living in the "Country of the Blind". The consequences of such a shift of awareness are unforeseeable, and one cannot help but sympathise with the considered statement by Professor H. H. Price that "psychical research is one of the most important branches of investigation which the human mind has undertaken";[16] that it seems likely "to throw entirely new light upon the nature of human personality and its position in the universe"; and that in time "it may transform the whole intellectual outlook upon which our present civilisation is based".[17]

These are strong words coming from an Oxford Professor of Philosophy, but I do not think they overstate the case. What they imply is a plea to make parapsychology, and more generally the study of what I called "confluential events", academically respectable and attractive to students, as a career or as an optional subject. Once there are as many bright researchers engaged in this field as there are now in the study of rat-behaviour, a breakthrough may be in sight.

In science fiction it is taken for granted that telepathic communication and psychokinetic manipulation of matter will become commonplace in the not-too-distant future; and science fiction has proved to be an astonishingly reliable prophet. Another of its favourite assumptions is that intelligent beings on other planets in the universe have advanced mastery of these methods. It is equally possible, however, that in this particular field we are an under-privileged species—together with our other handicaps. The grand design of evolution towards higher forms of unity-in-variety does not exclude biological freaks, nor pathological developments. I do not think the universe is a charitable institution, but we have to live in it and make the best of it. The limitations of our biological equipment may condemn us to the role of Peeping Toms at the keyhole of eternity. But at least let us take the stuffing out of the keyhole, which blocks even our limited view.

[AUTHOR'S NOTE *In the vast literature on contemporary parapsychology I have been particularly impressed by the writings of two women—Rosalind Heywood, to whom this book is dedicated, and Renée Haynes, author of* The Hidden Springs *and* Philosopher King, *and Editor of the* Journal of the Society for Psychical Research.

In writing the present essay about a field where angels fear to tread I have been treading with great caution, mostly confining myself to the experimental results of laboratory research, and omitting all so-called "anecdotal evidence"—that is, spontaneous manifestations of parapsychological phenomena in every-day life, which do not constitute evidence in the strict sense. Re-reading these pages at the proof stage, I felt that these self-imposed limitations resulted in a certain one-sidedness, and I asked Renée Haynes to restore the balance in the form of a Postscript. I am grateful to her for having done this, adding a flavour of Yin *to my austere* Yang. *A.K.*]

Postscript *By Renée Haynes*

Mr. Koestler has given us a lucid exposition of modern data as to space, time, matter, causality, neurophysiology and psychical research, out of which a remarkable synthesis emerges. His concept of "Janus-faced holons" may well prove as stimulating to our generation as was Bergson's *Elan Vital* to the thinkers of the early part of the century.

It is both gratifying and awe-inspiring to be asked to write an epilogue to such a work, especially as it provokes continual discussion. If this epilogue turns from time to time into argument I hope to be forgiven.

I have been impressed by Mr. Koestler's description of contemporary physics, with its infinitely abstract terms, its verifiable mathematical interactions, its invisible universe of energy dancing in predictable patterns and unpredictable flings, now here, now there, now nowhere and back again, exploding all the tidy network of Newtonian thought. It is, incidentally, a fascinating example of synchronicity that both physicists and para-psychologists should use the term psi to indicate what is still unknown; a curious verbal flash that may serve to indicate common ground between two disciplines.

For me, however, as for many others, the mathematical imagery which comes naturally to the numerate is much harder to comprehend, to relate to living experience, than is that given by the immediate impact of the senses. It is easier for the likes of us to think in the idiom of "ordinary" perception, that mysterious commonplace process, than in the idiom of algebraic formulae, whatever their truth and elegance. It is in the imagery of sight, hearing, touch, smell, temperature that paranormal cognition, like memory, often emerges into the conscious mind (often, though not always. There may be no more than a sudden impression that something has happened, even no more than an unaccountable impulse to act, to run out of a house which will shortly be bombed, to undertake a tedious cross-country journey to see a child at school, who turns out to be suddenly, dangerously ill*).

For this reason I should like to stress the value of spontaneous phenomena to psychical research. Baffling, unrepeatable, uniquely personal as such events may be, the fact that they do occur, that certain hallucinations, waking impressions, and vivid dreams can be correlated with objective happenings unknown to the person concerned, far away, long ago or not yet enacted, has repeatedly been made plain, both before and after systematic investigation began in the 1880's.

Even now, of course, such happenings are often dismissed as at best "anecdotal", or as old wives' tales, or as

* Cf. Ann Bridge, *Moments of Knowing*. London, 1970.

superstitious nonsense. In the same way, the perfectly accurate report that the inhabitants of St. Kilda only got colds when a ship came in was scouted by Dr. Johnson as contrary to all common sense, only to be accepted as a statement of fact when the germ theory of disease was established.

Many spontaneous instances of the paranormal—telepathic awareness, "crisis apparitions" perceived when the person "seen" was in danger or dying, the sudden onset of inexplicable pain at the time when it was being experienced unexpectedly by some loved individual far away—have been checked and verified by standards of evidence acceptable in a court of law. All this lends weight to the ever accumulating number of other cases which, though the narrator does not know it, fall into the same pattern, as Dr. Louisa Rhine* and others have pointed out.

Spontaneous extra-sensory perception pretty certainly occurs not only among humans, who have words with which to describe their experiences, but among animals, whose feelings can be gauged only by their appearance and behaviour. This is not always easy to interpret because so many of them have sensory powers that we lack. Adult rats, for instance, can "smell" X-rays.† Baby rodents of other kinds have been shown to communicate ultrasonically with their mothers, as dolphins of all ages sometimes do with one another. Thus, how easy—and how mistaken—it would have been to produce a paranormal explanation of the episode observed‡ in "the home of the American military attaché in an unidentified foreign capital". The family dog, howling and

* Cf. Louisa Rhine, *Hidden Channels of the Mind*. London, 1962, and G. W. Lambert's Foreword to Andrew MacKenzie, *Ghosts and Apparitions*. London, 1971.
† *Nature*, 8.xii.1962 and 6.ii.1965.
‡ *Daily Telegraph*, 11.v.1963, discussing a booklet issued by the State Department in Washington.

whining and "obviously in pain, appeared to be in heated combat with an enemy in the corner of the room". The floorboards were taken up and revealed "a radio device transmitting . . . all the conversations in the room". When switched on it produced a sound too high-pitched for the human ear to register, but tormenting to the dog.

All the same, there are well-authenticated instances of animal behaviour which seem only to make sense in terms of the paranormal. One sort concerns a domestic dog or cat which, taken in a closed basket by car or train over long distances, escapes from its new home and returns by the most direct cross-country route to its former surroundings. Odder still is the recent report in the French press of a dog belonging to a workman who left it with his family when he was sent off to another part of the country on a temporary assignment. The dog vanished from home and later, thin and exhausted, found its master in a place where it had never been before.

There are also frequent episodes in which dogs or cats seem to be aware of what is going on at a distance. I have already described* an instance personally known to me. That this was not an isolated case would appear from an article† in the *New Scientist* by Mr. W. J. Tarver, a practising veterinary surgeon, then Chairman of the Veterinarians Union. He wrote that "a gifted 10%" of dogs in boarding kennels "after being settled for a week or two become wildly excited at almost the exact moment when their owners begin the return journey from their holiday". It did not matter how far away those owners had gone. (It is odd that the percentage of dogs with such a gift should be so close to the percentage of humans who answered affirmatively the question put to them in the first Census of Hallucinations‡ held in

---

* Renée Haynes, *The Hidden Springs*. London, 1961.
† *New Scientist*, 24.x.1968.
‡ Report of the Census of Hallucinations. *Proc. SPR.*, Vol. X, 1894.

England: "Have you ever, while believing yourself completely awake, had a vivid impression . . . which, as far as you could discover, was not due to any external physical cause?" 17,000 replied, of whom nearly 1,700 said yes.) Love was the relevant stimulus to the exiled dogs longing for home. Fear triggered off another apparently paranormal response described by Mr. Tarver. "A bull," he said, "who had been operationally familiar with me used to bellow . . . the moment I turned off the road, so that his owner never failed to meet me," even when "I came in a new car" whose sounds could not have meant anything to the creature.

There is another parallel to be drawn between humans and other living beings. As J. D. Carthy* has said, "animals do not react automatically to a signal, but only if their motivation is high. A satiated animal will not react to a food call." Mr. Koestler has noted from a different angle (p. 128 et seq.) that this applies to humans as well as to animals, in ordinary life as under experimental conditions. Thus, in a busy street a small boy of a mechanical turn will notice makes of cars, an expert on town-planning the traffic flow, a woman anxious to cross with a tired child the collective impersonal disregard of drivers for those on foot. The same holds good of extrasensory perception. In this, too, people become vividly aware of what concerns themselves, and their personal feelings. To evoke an instant strong response in any living creature a signal, sensory or extra-sensory, has to be relevant; relevant to biological need, to emotional stress, to what Gerard Manley Hopkins called inscape.

This is of course why repeatable experiments in psychical research are so hard to achieve. The interest which leads people to take part in them is eroded by boring mechanical repetition, and the decline effect manifests itself, sooner or later in accordance with the tempera-

* *Nature*, 26.IV.1969.

ments, moods and personal relationships of those concerned Apart from the cumulative boredom they engender, moreover, experiments with cards, dice, lights and so on disregard the ambience within which the human mind works. As Professor H. H. Price* has pointed out, "Paranormal cognition is symbolic in an associative way; thus, Mr. Jones might be indicated in a dream or paranormal cognition by a lion because he lives near the Zoo, has a lion-like temperament or a relation called Leo. In card-guessing with an ordinary pack the percipient to score a direct hit must say literally 'the ten of spades'. The remark 'Ten honest men' [who call a spade a spade] would be thought totally irrelevant."

The first group of experiments at the Dream Laboratory of the Maimonides Medical Centre,† summarised on pp. 37–8, went some way towards obviating this difficulty, but their results, though suggestive, were hard to assess. This is partly because the power to visualise varies so vastly from one person to another. Some people have a photographic memory, some a selective one, some can recall the names but not the appearances of things. As well as all this everyone in the world perceives and expresses his feelings through a network of associations, images and symbols unique as his own self; some derive from his culture pattern, most from the events of his own individual life. A later series of experiments‡ using less specific targets—not just pictures but general *subjects* such as Far Eastern Religions, the Artistic Productions of Schizophrenics, The Birth of a Baby, all illustrated for the agent by sights and noises—seems to have bypassed some of

*Paper on Paranormal Cognition and Symbolism in *Image and Symbol, Colston Papers*, Vol. XII, London, 1960.
† M. Ullman and S. Krippner, *Dream Studies and Telepathy*. Parapsychology Foundation, New York, 1970.
‡ Stanley Krippner and Others, "A Long Distance 'Sensory Bombardment', a Study of ESP in Dreams." *JASPR.*, Vol. 65, No. 4, October 1971.

the earlier problems. It looks as if this method had really been successful in the telepathic communication of the mood, the quality, of an experience.

This matter of quality as contrasted with measurement in psychical research as in many other subjects seems to me to emerge with ever-increasing urgency. It cannot be ignored simply because it is so uncomfortable and so difficult to deal with. It is relevant to science, to philosophy, to the whole concept of synchronicity. Yet (because it is so much easier to accumulate and to quantify data than to reflect on their significance) quality and meaning, which matter most to men, tend to be brushed aside. That is one reason why this book is so valuable. It wrestles with meaning, integrates facts.

Yet I should like to stress the theme even more. The measurable, the calculable can serve quality, but differ from it in kind. "*Le son du cor le soir au fond des bois*", "The foam of perilous seas in faery lands forlorn", "a deepe and dazzling darknesse"—the phrases can be known and experienced instantaneously as meaning, but they are not susceptible of scientific analysis or of quantification. Similarly, you cannot have a ton of love (in spite of the way in which girls used to sign their letters), or a yard of hate or a gallon of numinous awe; but love and hate and awe are just as real as a ton of flour or a yard of linen or a gallon of petrol, more real indeed, because they have immediate significance, they are not simply means to ends like making bread or pillow cases or haste.

It is quality, meaning, that flashes like a shooting star through synchronicity; just as, oddly enough, at the other end of the psychophysical spectrum it flares through the phenomena of "poltergeist hauntings"* now believed to be the effect of profound chaotic human misery expressing itself in some psychokinetic mode not yet understood. Now grotesque, now terrifying, the noises,

* Cf. A. R. G. Owen, *Can We Explain the Poltergeist?* New York 1964.

the showers of stones, the smashed bottles, the exploding light bulbs, the violent inexplicable interference with electrical equipment* symbolise and convey more directly than words or music or painting the inner conflict and turmoil of the person around whom they occur.

Jung interprets these phenomena—like the detonations in Freud's bookcase—as extreme instances of "trans-psychic" causation. In everyday life, they are of course manifested in less dramatic ways. I decide to write a sentence and the electrical functioning of my brain, the motor functioning of my muscles carry out that decision through a traceable linked chain of physical causes, but it was my decision that set the process going. It is possible, moreover, that such decisions may have direct effects on biological processes not in physical contact with the body of the decision-maker, as suggested in a recent paper by John L. Randall on "Psi Phenomena and Biological Theory",† which cites references to experimental work-testing psychokinetic effects on enzyme activity, on para-mecia, on plant growth, and on the healing of lesions in mice. He provides, incidentally, the following neat general definition: "A psi-phenomenon is said to have occurred whenever information is transferred to a physical system without the use of any known form of physical energy."

We might thus distinguish between different levels: conscious decision-making; phenomena of the poltergeist type engendered in the sub-conscious strata of the psyche; and lastly synchronicity and meaningful coincidences produced by mind operating on yet another, inconceivable level.

In this connection I think I must take issue with Mr.

---

* "The Rosenheim Poltergeist Case", A Paper read by Dr. Hans Bender, the 11th Annual Convention of the Parapsychological Association at Freiburg, September 1968.

See also *JSPR.*, Vol. 46, No. 750, December 1970.

† *SPR*, Vol. 46, No. 749, September 1971.

Koestler as to the "oceanic feeling" and "the dominant concept" that "all is One and One is all" which "echoes through the writings of Christian mystics" (p. 108). I am sure that this happens, and that, as he writes, it is an upward turn of the spiral from the symbiotic awareness of the child, the golden "dream time" of the primitive. But I do not think all mystics, Christian or otherwise, share this dominant concept, or the sense of oneness with the *anima mundi* that underlies it. They are on fire with almost intolerable gladness, but they are not swallowed up in it. There can be no perception without a perceiver; and contemplatives retain their selves enough to perceive as they rejoice. It is as if the sunset, or the mountain range or night of stars that set them gazing in wonder showed itself to be alive and gazing back at them.

There is on record a sober remark of Francis Bacon, lawyer, statesman, essayist and early scientist, who devised for the first time in England experimental methods for testing paranormal cognition. "I had rather believe all the fables of the *Talmud* and the *Alcoran* than that this Universal Frame were without a Mind"; a mind which is more than a mathematical computer and more than some vast automatic nervous system animating all that exists, as efficient and as unconscious of itself as a healthy digestion.

REFERENCES

1. THE ABC OF ESP (pages 11–49)

1. Eysenck, (1957), p. 131 f. 2. Ibid., p. 108. 3. Naumov (1970), p. 54.
4. Quoted by *Newsletter of the Parapsychology Foundation, Inc.*, Vol. 10,
No. 6, November–December, 1963, and by Heywood (1967), pp.
57–8. 5. Quoted by Heywood (1967), p. 58. 6. Quoted by Burt
(1967), p. 75 n. 7. Weaver (1963), p. 361. 8. 20.VIII.1970, p. 367.
9. Burt (1968), p. 59. 10. Weaver (1963), p. 267. 11. Ibid., pp. 361–2.
12. Ibid., p. 361. 13. *Proc. SPR*, Vol. II, pp. 189–200. 14. *Proc. SPR*,
Vol. XXIX, Part LXXII, 23.II.1916, p. 64. 15. *Proc. SPR*, Vol.
XXXIV, Part XCII, December 1924, p. 212. 16. Murray (1952).
17. L. Rhine (1957), pp. 131–2. 18. Broad (1949), pp. 291–309.
19. L. Rhine (1957), p. 19. 19a. Ibid., p. 17. 20. Ibid., p. 19. 21. Ibid.,
p. 166. 22. Ibid., p. 166. 23. Schmidt (1969), p. 99. 24. Schmidt
(1970), p. 175. 25. Ibid., p. 181. 26. "ESP by any Other Name
Would Smell", *New Scientist*, 20.VIII.1970, p. 367.

2. THE PERVERSITY OF PHYSICS (pages 50–81)

1. Oppenheimer (1966), p. 40. 2. Heisenberg (1969), pp. 63–4, 115.
3. Russell (1927), pp. 163, 165. 4. Quoted by Burt (1967), p. 80. 5.
Eddington (1928), introduction. 6. Quoted by Heisenberg (1969),
pp. 101 et seq. 7. Heisenberg, op. cit., p. 113. 8. Quoted by Burt
(1968), p. 36. 9. Pauli (1952), p. 164. 10. Quoted by Hardy (1965),
p. 256. 11. Burt (1967), p. 80. 12. Margenau (1967), p. 209. 13. Jeans
(1937), pp. 122 f. 14. Burt (1967), pp. 80–1. 15. Gardner (1967), pp.
240–1. 16. In *Telephone Poles and Other Poems*, 1963. 17. Firsoff (1967),
pp. 102–3. 18. Ibid., pp. 105–6. 19. Gamow (1966), p. 132. 20. Ibid.,
pp. 121–2. 21. 10.XI.1956. 22. Reichenbach (1956). 23. Dobbs
(1965), pp. 261–2. 24. Margenau (1967), p. 217. 25. Quoted by Dobbs
(1965), p. 303. 26. Dobbs (1965), pp. 303 and 305. 27. Eccles (1953),
pp. 271–2. 28. Koestler (1945), p. 207. 29. Ibid., p. 227. 30. Eccles
(1953), p. 276–7. 31. Ibid., pp. 283–5. 32. Ibid., p. 279. 33. Firsoff
(1967), p. 52. 34. Burt (1968), pp. 34–5. 35. Dobbs (1965), pp. 333
et seq. 36. Gamow (1966), p. 111.

3. SERIALITY AND SYNCHRONICITY (pages 82–104)

1. Jung (1960), p. 420. 2. Kammerer (1919), p. 25. 3. Ibid., p. 27.
4. Ibid., p. 24. 5. Ibid., p. 36. 6. Koestler (1971), Appendix I. 7.
Kammerer (1919), p. 93. 8. Ibid., p. 165. 9. Ibid., p. 456. 10.
Margenau (1967), p. 218. 11. Jung–Pauli (1952). 12. Ibid., p. 164.
13. Jung (1960), p. 317. 14. Jaffé (1967), p. 264. 15. Jaffé, ed. (1963),
p. 152. 16. Jung (1960), p. 318. 17. Moser (1950), p. 257. 18. Jung
(1960), p. 438. 19. Ibid., p. 159 f. 20. Ibid., p. 318. 21. Ibid., p. 441.

22. Ibid., p. 511. 23. Ibid., p. 435. 24. Ibid., p. 445. 25. Ibid., p. 511. 26. Ibid., p. 436. 27. Ibid., p. 438. 28. Ibid., p. 440. 29. Ibid., pp. 444–5. 30. Jaffé (1967), p. 267. 31. Quoted by LeShan (1969), p. 82. 32. Hook (1959). 33. Jung (1960), p. 514. 34. Ibid., pp. 515 f. 35. Hardy (1965), p. 242.

4. JANUS (pages 105–120)

1. Pico della Mirandola (1557), p. 40 f. 2. Kepler (1609), cap. 28. 3. Ibid. 4. Schopenhauer (1850), p. 219. 5. Ibid., p. 224. 6. Ibid., p. 225. 7. Koestler (1964), p. 228. 8. Whitehead (1934), p. 181. 9. Koestler (1968), p. 260. 10. Bleibtreu (1968), pp. 215–19. 11. v. Bertalanffy (1952), p. 112. 12. Koestler (1967), pp. 190–2, 242.

5. THE COUNTRY OF THE BLIND (pages 121–140)

1. Grey Walter (1969), p. 37. 2. Grey Walter (1969). 3. Haynes (1970), p. 364. 4. Black (1969). 5. Margenau (1967), pp. 223–4. 6. Broad (1949), pp. 291–309. 7. Quoted by Dobbs (1967), p. 239. 8. Dobbs (1967), p. 239. 9. Hayes (1962), p. 161. 10. Burt (1968), pp. 50, 58–9. 11. Burt (1962), p. 86. 12. Waddington (1957), pp. 180 seq. 13. Quoted by Sciama (1959), p. 99. 14. Ibid. 15. Pico della Mirandola (1557), p. 40 f. 16. Price (1949), pp. 105–13. 17. Heywood (1959), p. 212.

BIBLIOGRAPHY

BALFOUR, the Countess of, *Proc. SPR.*, Vol. 52, Part 189, February 1960.

BATEMAN, F. See Soal, S. G.

BELOFF, J., and EVANS, L., *J. of the SPR.*, 1961, *41*, 41–6.

VON BERTALANFFY, L., *Problems of Life.* New York, 1952.

BIRCHALL, J. See Guthrie, M.

BLACK, S., *Mind and Body.* London, 1969.

BLEIBTREU, J., *The Parable of the Beast.* New York, 1968.

BOHM, D., *Quantum Theory.* London, 1951.

BRIER, R. See Rhine, J. B. (1968).

BROAD, C. D., *Philosophy*, Vol. XXIV, 1949, pp. 291–309.

——*Lectures on Psychical Research.* London, 1962.

——*J. of SPR*, December, 1970.

BROWN, G. Spencer, "Statistical Significance in Psychical Research", *Nature*, July 25, 1953.

——*Probability and Scientific Inference.* London 1957.

BURT, Sir Cyril, in *The Scientist Speculates—An Anthology of Partly Baked Ideas.* See Good, I. J., ed.

——"Psychology and Parapsychology" in *Science and ESP.* See Smythies, J. R., ed.

——*Psychology and Psychical Research. The Seventeenth Frederick W. H. Myers Memorial Lecture.* London: SPR, 1968.

CARINGTON, W., *Telepathy.* London, 1945.

CHAUVIN, R., and GENTHON, J., *Zeitschrift für Parapsychologie und Grenzgebiete der Psychologie*, 1965, 8, 140–7.

CUMMINGS, Geraldine, *Swan on a Black Sea.* London: 1st ed. 1965; 2nd ed. 1970.

DOBBS, A., *Proc. SPR*, Vol. 57, Part 197, August 1965.

——"The Feasibility of a Physical Theory of ESP" in *Science and ESP.* See Smythies, J. R., ed.

ECCLES, Sir John, *The Neurophysiological Basis of Mind.* Oxford, 1953.

EDDINGTON, A. S., *The Nature of the Physical World.* Cambridge, 1928.

——*The Philosophy of Physical Science.* Cambridge, 1939.

EVANS, L. See Beloff, J.

EYSENCK, H. J., *Sense and Nonsense in Psychology.* Penguin, 1957.

FIRSOFF, V. A., *Life, Mind and Galaxies.* Edinburgh and London, 1967.

FISK, G. W., and WEST, D. J., "Psychokinetic Experiments with a Single Subject", *Newsletter of the Parapsychology Foundation, Inc.*, Nov.–Dec., 1957.

FRASER, J. T., ed., *The Voices of Time.* London, 1968.

FREUD, S., "Psychoanalysis and Telepathy", *Gesammelte Werke*, Vol. XVII. London, 1941.

FURTH, H. P., *New Yorker*, November 10, 1956.

GAMOW, G., *Thirty Years That Shook Physics*. New York, 1966.

GARDNER, M., *The Ambidextrous Universe*. London, 1967.

GENTHON, J. See Chauvin, R.

GOOD, I. J., ed. *The Scientist Speculates—An Anthology of Partly Baked Ideas*. London, 1962.

GREY WALTER, W., *Observations on Man, His Frame, His Duty and His Expectations*. Cambridge, 1969.

——*The Evoked Potentials* (ed. Wm. Cobb and C. Morocutt). Elsevier, 1967.

GUERNEY, E., MYERS, F. W. H., and PODMORE, F., *Phantasms of the Living*. London, 1886.

GUTHRIE, M., and BIRCHALL, J., *Proc. SPR.*, Vol. II, pp. 24–42, and Vol. III, pp. 424–52.

HANSEL, C. E. M., *ESP: A Scientific Evaluation*. London, 1966.

HARDY, Sir Alister, *The Living Stream*. London, 1965.

HAYES, J. S., in *The Scientist Speculates—An Anthology of Partly Baked Ideas*. See Good, I. J., ed.

HAYNES, Renée, *The Hidden Springs*. London, 1961.

——*J. of SPR.*, Vol. XLV, No. 745, September 1970.

HEISENBERG, W., *Der Teil und das Ganze*. München, 1969.

HEYWOOD, Rosalind, *The Sixth Sense*. London, 1959.

——"Notes on Changing Mental Climates and Research into ESP" in *Science and ESP*. See Smythies, J. R., ed.

HOOK, S., "Conscience and Consciousness in Japan", *Commentary*, January 1959.

JAFFÉ, A., ed., *Memories, Dreams, Reflections by C. G. Jung*. London, 1963.

——"C. G. Jung and Parapsychology" in *Science and ESP*. See Smythies, J. R., ed.

JEANS, Sir James, *The Mysterious Universe*. Cambridge, 1937.

JUNG, C. G., Preface to German ed. of S. E. White, *Das Uneinge-schränkte Weltall*. Zürich, 1948.

——"Synchronizität als ein Prinzip akausaler Zusammenhänge" in Jung–Pauli, *Naturerklärung und Psyche. Studien aus dem C. G. Jung-Institut, Zürich, IV*, 1952. See also Pauli, W.

——*The Structure and Dynamics of the Psyche, Collected Works*, Vol. VIII. Tr. Hull, R. F. C. London, 1960.

——*Memories, Dreams, Reflections by C. G. Jung*. See Jaffé, A., ed.

KAMMERER, Paul, *Das Gesetz der Serie*. Deutsche Verlags-Anstalt Stuttgart-Berlin, 1919.

KEPLER, J., *De Stella Nova*, 1609. *Opera Omnia*, ed. Ch. Frisch. Frankofurti et Erlangae, 1858–1871.

KOESTLER, A., *The Yogi and the Commissar*. London, 1945.

——*Insight and Outlook*. London, 1949.

——*The Sleepwalkers*. London, 1959.

——*The Act of Creation*. London, 1964.

——*The Lotus and the Robot*. London, 1960.

——*The Ghost in the Machine*. London, 1967.

——*Drinkers of Infinity*. London, 1968.

——*The Case of the Midwife Toad*. London, 1971.

——and SMYTHIES, J. R., ed. *Beyond Reductionism—New Perspectives in the Life Sciences. The Alpbach Symposium*. London, 1969.

KRIPPNER, S., and ULLMAN, M., *Proc. Parapsychological Association*, No. 5, 1968.

LeSHANN, L., *J. of Transpersonal Psychology*. Autumn, 1969.

LODGE, Sir O., *Proc. SPR.*, Vol. II, pp. 189–200.

MARGENAU, H., "ESP in the Framework of Modern Science" in *Science and ESP*. See Smythies, J. R., ed.

della MIRANDOLA, Pico, *Opera Omnia*. Basle, 1557.

MOSER, F., *Spuk*. Baden bei Zürich, 1950.

MURRAY, G., "Presidential Address", *Proc. SPR.*, Vol. XLIX, Part 181, November 1952. Reprinted in *Science and ESP*—see Smythies, J. R., ed.

MYERS, F. W. H. See Guerney, E.

NAUMOV, E. K., *J. of Paraphysics*, Vol. IV, No. 2, 1970.

OPPENHEIMER, J. R., *Science and the Human Understanding*. New York, 1966.

PAULI, W., "Der Einfluss Archetypischer Vorstellungen auf die Bildung Naturwissenschaftlicher Theorien bei Kepler" in Jung-Pauli, *Naturerklärung und Psyche*. See Jung, 1952.

PODMORE, F. See Guerney, E.

PRATT, J. G. See Rhine, J. B., 1957.

PRICE, H. H., *Hibbert J.*, Vol. XLVII, pp. 105–13, 1949.

——"Psychical Research and Human Personality" in *Science and ESP*. See Smythies, J. R., ed.

PRZIBRAM, H., "Paul Kammerer als Biologe". *Monistische Monatshefte*, November 1926.

REICHENBACH, H., *The Direction of Time*. California and Cambridge, 1956.

RHINE, J. B., *The Reach of the Mind*. New York, 1947.

——and PRATT, J. G., *Parapsychology—Frontier Science of the Mind*. Springfield, Ill., 1957.

——and BRIER, R., *Parapsychology Today*. Durham, N.C., 1968.

RHINE, L., *ESP in Life and Lab*. London, 1957.

——*Hidden Channels of the Mind*. London, 1961.

RUSSELL, B., *An Outline of Philosophy*. London, 1927.

SCHMEIDLER, Gertrude, *Extra-Sensory Perception*. Atherton Press, 1969.

SCHMIDT, H., *J. of Parapsychology*, Vol. XXXIII, No. 2, June 1969.

——*J. of Parapsychology*, Vol. XXXIII, No. 4, December 1969a.

——*J. of Parapsychology*, Vol. XXXIV, No. 3, September 1970.

——*J. of Parapsychology*, Vol. XXXIV, No. 4, December 1970a.

——*New Scientist*, June 24, 1971.

SCHOPENHAUER, A., *Sämtliche Werke*, Vol. VIII. Stuttgart, 1850.

SCIAMA, D. W., *The Unity of the Universe*. London, 1959.

SIDGWICK, Mrs. Henry, *Proc. SPR.*, Vol. XXXIV, Part XCII, December 1924, p. 212.

SINCLAIR, U., *Mental Radio*. Foreword by Albert Einstein. Springfield, Illinois, 1930.

SMYTHIES, J. R., ed., *Science and ESP*. London, 1967.

——See Koestler (1969).

SOAL, S. G., and BATEMAN, F., *Modern Experiments in Telepathy*. London, 1954.

THOMSON, Sir G., *Nature*, Vol. 187, pp. 837–41, 1960.

THOULESS, R. H., and WIESNER, B. P., *Proc. SPR.*, Vol. XLVIII, pp. 177–96.

——*J. of Parapsychology*, Vol. XII, pp. 192–212.

TYRRELL, G. N. M., *The Personality of Man*. Penguin, 1947.

ULLMAN, M. See Krippner, S.

UPDIKE, J., "Cosmic Gall" in *Telephone Poles and Other Poems*. New York, 1963.

VERRALL, Mrs. A. W., *Proc. SPR.*, Vol. XXIX, Part LXXII, 23.11.1916, p. 64.

WADDINGTON, C. H., *The Strategy of the Genes*. London, 1957.

WEAVER, W., *Lady Luck and the Theory of Probability*. New York, 1963.

WELLS, H. G., *The Country of the Blind*. London, 1911.

WEST, D. J. See Fisk, G. W.

WHITEHEAD, A. N., *Nature and Life*. Cambridge, 1934.

WHITROW, G. J., "Time and the Universe" in *The Voices of Time*. See Fraser, J. T., ed.

WIESNER, B. P. See Thouless, R. H.

INDEX

Francis Hitching
Earth Magic £1

This book explores one of the last great mysteries of civilization . . .
What was the purpose of the stone circles, dolmens, hill 'forts', which are
scattered along the Atlantic seaboard of northern Europe, from
Scandinavia to Brittany? What inspired megalithic people to erect
monuments with almost unimaginable labour and infinite precision?

Francis Hitching's search for information about the elusive 'earth magic'
has led him down some strange paths: from astronomy, geometry and
higher mathematics to UFOs, ESP and dragon lore. This is an absorbing
investigation of a central overwhelming question: *is there indeed a
hidden force that our ancestors knew and used, but that we have lost?*

John Livingstone Lowes
The Road to Xanadu £1.95
– a study in the ways of the imagination

600 pages representing years of brilliant research, conducting the reader
along the highways of Coleridge's imagination and memory to meet with
'alligators and albatrosses . . . spectres and slimy seas, and the
observatory at Pekin.'

'Remarkable analysis of the way in which Coleridge's imagination worked
to create *The Ancient Mariner* and *Kubla Khan*'
TIMES LITERARY SUPPLEMENT

'A superb piece of criticism and literary detection' J. B. PRIESTLEY